# R A W

*charlie trotter & roxanne klein*

PHOTOGRAPHY BY TIM TURNER    WINE NOTES BY JASON SMITH

# R A W

TEN SPEED PRESS

Berkeley | Toronto

# table of contents

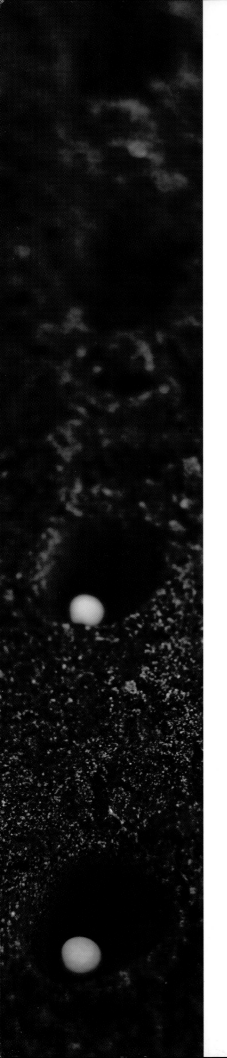

# INTRODUCTION

*by charlie trotter*

For several years, Michael and Roxanne Klein had been regularly flying from San Francisco to Chicago just to have dinner (my kind of people!) at the restaurant. Then, in 1999, they began to challenge my culinary abilities by requesting raw-food menus. Before that time, they had first enjoyed our vegetable tasting menu, and later had begun asking for the kitchen's version of vegan cuisine. Suddenly, they started to push all the way: "What," they wanted to know, "could we do with raw and living foods?" In those days, fulfilling the demand seemed fairly straightforward: either cut everything thinly, chop it finely, or purée it; add a few herbs, a vinaigrette, maybe a spice mixture, or possibly some chile; and serve it up. Raw cuisine appeared to be as simple as that.

But like most things that seem simple on the surface, the preparation of raw and living foods isn't simple at all. It is instead quite complex and requires serious study to learn the basic properties of foods and how foods act when handled in various ways. For example, when you soak nuts and legumes to sprout them,

9

you not only obtain maximum nutritional value, but you also achieve superior flavor. Or if you marinate certain vegetables for six to eight hours or more, you break down their undesirable starchiness completely.

You also learn that having a few specific pieces of equipment, while not essential, can help you produce utterly sublime results. A dehydrator greatly concentrates flavor, at times delivering a product that almost tastes roasted. A juicer yields glorious elixirs for serving as soups or beverages, while a high-speed blender will transform nearly any fruit or vegetable into a smooth and silky purée.

As I began to learn from the Kleins and to investigate on my own, I started to see some magnificent possibilities. This is a way of eating that embraces healthful living, of course, but it is also a wonderfully exciting approach to food preparation that opens up fresh ways to celebrate flavor and texture. I have long viewed vegetables as the most compelling flavor on any plate, and they have been a hallmark of my cuisine. Now, however, preparing raw foods presents me with exciting new roads of exploration.

I believe that in the not-too-distant future all serious chefs and home cooks will have a decent understanding of how to prepare raw and living foods and have at least several raw dishes in their repertoire. I began offering a vegetable tasting menu at Charlie Trotter's in the mid-1980s. After the Kleins provoked my interest

in raw foods, I introduced some raw dishes to the menu, and our diners responded with great enthusiasm. My primary objectives with all food—raw and cooked— are flavor and purity, and although my appreciation of the aesthetic possibilities of raw foods is foremost, I am also interested in expanding my culinary arsenal. Thus, it becomes effortless to incorporate this new and intriguing style of eating into how I communicate gastronomically.

In this collaboration, Roxanne and I have tried to fuse our common sensibilities of flavor and purity. We have also attempted to take our separate expressions and marry them into a coherent whole. The idea is to share an exceptional and exciting way to approach food, and then to elevate the possibilities. You need risk takers with a sense of purpose to move ideas forward. Michael and Roxanne Klein are so full of commitment and profound passion about the prospects of raw and living foods that they are genuinely inspiring. Use this book as a guide and starting point, and there is a strong chance you will enter a brave new world of eating!

*by roxanne klein*

In 1996, my husband, Michael, and I were busy doing research on a cookbook. I had decided that I wanted to create a volume that would present vegan versions of various cultural flavor models, and in pursuit of that goal, we went to Thailand to study the local cuisine. While we were there, we met up with several friends, among them actor and activist Woody Harrelson.

Every evening, our group would sit down to a fantastic feast of Thai vegetarian curries, noodles, and rice dishes. Woody, however, would always order a bowl of fruit or a green papaya salad. We tried to get him to sample the wonderful cooked dishes we were eating, but he always declined. Eventually we pressed him for an answer on why he turned down such delicious Thai meals, and he told us that he ate only raw foods. After more prodding, he explained the reasons why he maintained a diet of raw fruits and vegetables. Michael and I found the philosophy interesting and decided to delve more deeply into it.

When we returned home, we ordered several books on raw foods. The material was intriguing and convinced us that we should try this new way of eating soon. We were planning to spend a month that summer in Hawaii, and our first thought was that it would be warm there, so we wouldn't be cold without our usual cooked foods. Our second thought was that a lot of great fruits grow in the Islands. We made the decision to eat only raw fruits and salads for our month away.

At the end of that month, we felt healthier than we ever had in the past. We were sleeping two hours less each night, and our energy level was the best it had been in our lives. We were exercising several hours a day, and the positive impact on our bodies was undeniable. We have been eating raw since that trip.

I eat this way for two reasons: I love the sensual experience of eating foods in their natural state, and I love the way eating them makes me feel. I am not a doctor or trained nutritionist. I rely on listening to my body and how I feel. At the same time, the health arguments for raw foods are compelling. Many experts believe living or raw foods are the key to good health and longevity. They are the foods that have nourished our bodies for over 3,950,000 years of the roughly 4,000,000-year evolution of the species. Simply put, raw foods supplied everything we needed for almost all of our evolutionary development.

The most important health aspect of eating living or raw foods is enzyme preservation. Enzymes help you digest food, and they act as catalysts for every metabolic reaction in your body. Without them, there can be no cell division, energy production, or brain activity. In addition, no vitamins or hormones can do their work, nor can your immune system.

Every food contains the perfect mix of enzymes to digest it completely. These are called food enzymes. Nature in her never-ending perfection sees that all food, whether flesh, fruit, or vegetable, decomposes and returns to the earth from which it came. Cooking foods above 118°F destroys their natural enzymes, forcing our bodies to generate the enzymes necessary to digest them. Two main problems occur because of this enzyme destruction. First, your body cannot produce enzymes in perfect combinations to metabolize your foods as completely as the food enzymes created by nature do. This results in partially digested fats, proteins, and starches that can clog your body's intestinal tract and arteries.

The Eskimos are a remarkable example of the transformative power of enzymes. The word *Eskimo* means "one who eats raw." While living for centuries on a diet that consisted primarily of raw whale or seal blubber, Eskimos developed no arteriosclerosis and experienced almost no incidence of heart disease, stroke, or high blood pressure. Established nutritional doctrine would predict a high rate of these ailments given the diet, but even blubber will digest itself completely if it is not cooked since its enzymes are intact. Once you heat even the finest olive oil above 118°F, you will not be able to digest it completely.

More important, many authorities believe that eating cooked foods depletes our finite enzyme reserve. Proof of this effect is that an eighty-five-year-old has only one-thirtieth the enzyme activity level of an eighteen-year-old. In other words, your enzyme reserve is slowly exhausted over a lifetime of eating cooked foods.

I have used the terms *raw foods* and *living foods* interchangeably, but there is a subtle difference. Living foods have both their "life force" and their food enzymes available. Raw foods, in contrast, even though they have not been heated to above 118°F, do not necessarily have their food enzymes available. For example, nuts and seeds have enzyme inhibitors that prevent them from growing into a plant or tree. Only after they have been sprouted will these enzyme inhibitors dissolve away. This means that unsprouted nuts and seeds are almost as difficult to digest as cooked ones. Some cooked foods, such as miso, have been cultured with living beneficial bacteria. If the miso has not been heat processed after culturing, it is considered a living food and can be digested easily. In other words, not all raw foods are living, and not all living foods are raw.

My journey along the road to creating a raw cuisine began early in life. I am a fifth-generation Californian. My ancestors were pioneers, driven by the prospect of a new experience. The first four generations were all farmers in the Central Valley, and I spent much of my childhood on my grandparents' farm. They raised organic crops, and they ate what they grew.

My grandfather taught me about the lusciousness of produce in its natural state. When we would be walking around the farm, he would often ask me what I smelled. I can remember saying "peaches and strawberries," to which he would say, "That's what we'll harvest today." This is how I choose all of the ingredients that I use. If an ingredient does not have an aroma that conjures up a delicious taste, then it was probably harvested at the wrong time, is out of season, or was not grown organically with care. Spending time on my grandparents' farm taught me about the flavors of fruits and vegetables in season—about how delectable a perfectly ripe peach, still slightly warm from the sun, can be. Such experiences are what I have drawn on to originate dishes that are expressions of the flavors and textures of the seasons.

My raw cuisine is about discovering the inherent sensuality of each ingredient in its natural state, and then highlighting it in the final dish. In developing the cuisine, I had to learn how to use a different set of ingredients to achieve various textures and degrees of richness, often relying on a dehydrator for a desired result. I mastered culturing my own cheeses, using nut bases rather than milk. In the absence of heat for intensifying or melding flavors, I had to come up with ways to rebalance or resequence each dish to showcase its individual ingredients. In some of my recipes I have used ingredients, including hundred-year-old balsamic vinegar, maple syrup, and cocoa powder, that are not

raw. But I have added them in only very small amounts and only when using them truly elevates the sensuality of the final dish.

When Michael and I started Roxanne's, we wanted to share the sensual experience of eating this way with others. We have been overwhelmed by the warm response from our community. Part of our success is due to fact that we are not trying to tell people how they should eat. I think it is presumptuous for anyone to tell others how they should live their lives. Eating should always be a celebration, and insisting that anyone eat a certain way takes the sensuality and joy out of the experience. In that spirit, Charlie and I have created the recipes for this book, and we hope that you will enjoy using them.

---

I acknowledge my friend and chef de cuisine, Stephanie Valentine, for her incredible support. I also want to acknowledge my husband, Michael, for his help in making my dreams come true! Also, thanks to my toughest recipe testers: Alex, Raja, Warren, and Lillian.

Most of the ingredients in this book have followed a single natural path: seed, soil, harvest, table. Wine generally travels this same path, making it the ideal accompaniment to nearly every raw dish. Eating raw and living foods is about reconnecting with the earth, and sipping a glass of fine wine at mealtime strengthens that connection.

All food and wine pairing is about balance. It is an attempt to marry the flavors and textures of a dish with the many tastes and aromas found in wine. In the perfect pairing, neither the food nor the wine dominates, and the two together deliver a level of contrast and balance to the diner that neither could achieve alone.

White wines readily complement raw cuisine, and thus account for roughly 70 percent of the suggested pairings in *Raw*. Most of these whites are crisp, light- or medium-bodied wines that have seen little or no oak aging. Green vegetables and herbs and citrus vinaigrettes are just some of the ingredients that shine when teamed with such wines. Several grapes, including Riesling, Sauvignon Blanc, Albarino, and Grüner

Veltliner, are natural allies of raw foods, promoting the bright, mineral flavors of the ingredients with which they are paired.

But red wines can also be sound options. Preparations with fuller, meatier flavors, such as dishes containing mushrooms and "cheese," pair exceptionally well with Pinot Noir, Grenache, and Sangiovese. These reds, like the whites, can handle the brighter flavors and higher acidity of raw foods.

When pairing wine with raw food, always look at the structural components and weight of the dish before concentrating on the flavors. Your first job is to select a wine that will balance and harmonize with the acidity, sweetness, and body of the dish. This establishes a sound pairing without any off tastes or other negative results. Only after this foundation is laid should you begin to focus on the flavors.

There are two distinct directions you can take when pairing flavors. You can either complement the dish with similar flavors or contrast it with opposite and different tastes to add another dimension to the overall experience. It is much simpler, and safer, to go the complement route. In a dish with apples and pears, for example, find a wine that has these same aromas and you're off to a great start. A pairing based on contrast might put together a fruity red wine with an earthy mushroom preparation. But contrast is much riskier, and while the potential for a fantastic match is possible, the chance for disaster exists as well. The most

important thing to remember is to be adventurous and not to be afraid to make mistakes. You can always open another bottle of wine!

Raw cuisine is closely linked to the sustainable agriculture movement and the use of organic products. Because of this, many wines recommended in this book are organic. Some wine producers, such as Nicolas Joly and Nikolaihof, go beyond everyday organic agriculture rules. They practice biodynamic wine production, a kind of highly refined organic farming that follows the natural rhythms dictated by lunar and cosmic influences. By growing their grapes in this completely natural environment they hope to create greater individuality in their vineyards.

Living and raw foods are about pure, natural ingredients that have experienced little alteration. Wine, at its most basic, is also an unadulterated creation, never rising above 118°F during its production. We all should be thankful that wine meets the strict standards that govern raw cuisine, for it allows us to uncork a bottle of this favorite nectar to enjoy alongside the wonderful dishes that follow.

JASON SMITH, SOMMELIER, CHARLIE TROTTER'S

# notes from the farmer

Chefs like Roxanne Klein and Charlie Trotter exemplify the mastery of the culinary arts. They take the humble vegetable, arguably the most complex and interesting of all ingredients, and apply their magic to create amazing results. The reason that The Chef's Garden and other organic farms similar to it exist is in large part because of these two chefs and others like them.

The primary goal of organic farmers is to grow the most flavorful vegetables and fruits possible. The key to realizing this goal is to cultivate them in accordance with the rhythms of nature. Many farmers have discovered that the best way to produce good-tasting harvests is to go back to the way vegetables were grown by their ancestors, before the advent of so many damaging chemicals. This means taking care of the soil through the use of cover crops, compost, and crop rotation. Farmers are the stewards of the land, and we have an obligation to take good care of it by applying the principles of sustainable agriculture. Part of that responsibility also involves seeking out chefs to find out what we can grow for them.

Teamwork between chefs and farmers is critical to the continuing expansion of organic farming, and at The Chef's Garden, we are constantly encouraging this important relationship. In our 2003 experimental gardens, we have some five hundred different species growing, many of them European or American native plants suggested by chefs who have visited the farm. Indeed, it is common for us to receive seeds from a chef for a plant of particular interest to him or her.

They are usually for a vegetable variety long ago abandoned by commercial growers because it had a low yield. Chefs also sample what we grow and assist us in determining which plants should go into production in coming years. We have been extremely fortunate to have some excellent teammates who are as passionate about sustainable agriculture as we are. These are people who do not measure success by ton per acre, but rather by flavor per mouthful. Keeping that in mind, we pick and ship our vegetables today and tomorrow they are on the dinner table.

As part of our efforts to promote sounder agricultural practices, we have established a learning center at The Chef's Garden. The center welcomes chefs to come and walk through our gardens, select any plants that appeal to them, and then experiment with them in our kitchen. We also invite chefs to browse in our extensive library of agricultural and culinary works, to offer classes, and to participate in our project to encourage children worldwide to eat more nutritiously.

Of course, we are not alone in the effort to advance the principles of sustainable agriculture. A growing number of farmers across the country are as interested as we are in producing high-quality, good-tasting, safe products for the table. At the same time, more and more people are beginning to realize how important it is to support agriculture that harms neither the land nor the consumers who depend on its harvests.

LEE JONES, FARMER-OWNER, THE CHEF'S GARDEN

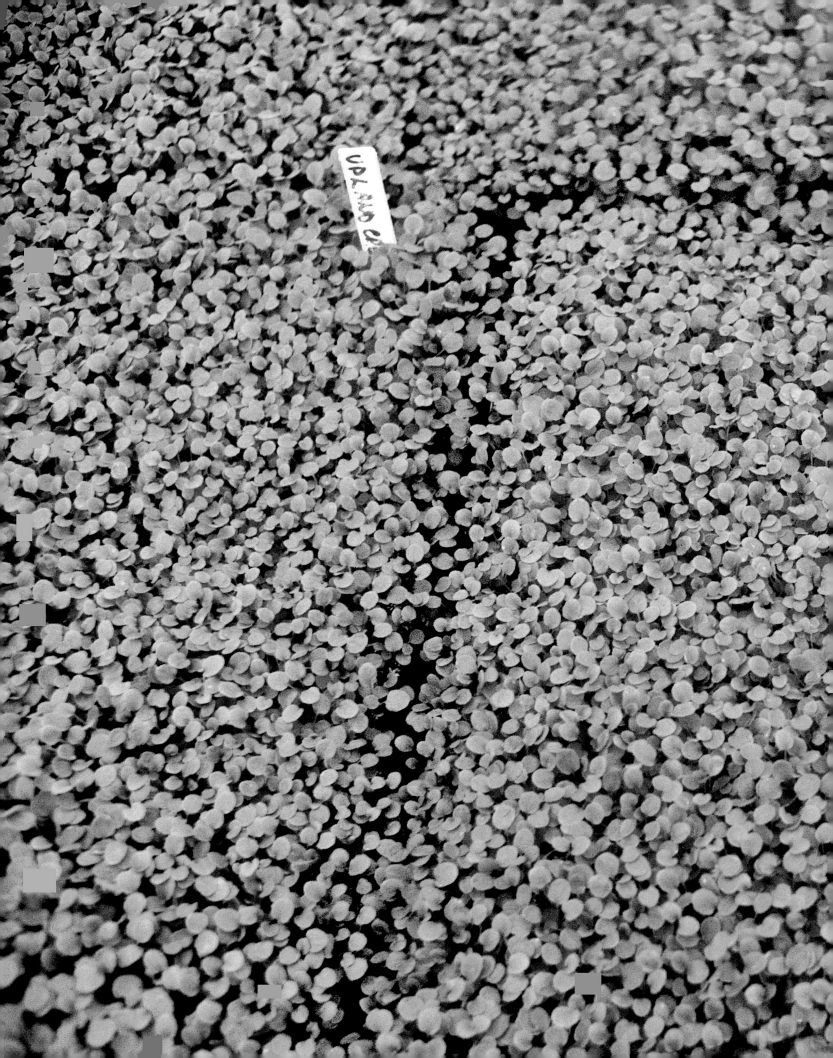

# APPETIZERS

# Wakame Sushi Rolls

*This unique sushi works perfectly as a plated first course or a passed canapé. The carrots, cucumber, and daikon serve as superb textural foils for the rice, while the Wasabi Mayonnaise provides a wonderful creaminess and the appropriate heat. A drizzle of shoyu caps off the preparation.*

**Method**—*To make the Wakame Salad:* Combine all the ingredients in a bowl and toss to mix. Let stand for 1 hour. Drain, reserving the liquid. Dice ¹/₄ cup of the salad to use for adding to the rice; set aside the remaining drained salad for adding to the sushi rolls.

*To make the Sushi Rice:* In a food processor, combine the parsnip and pine nuts and pulse until ricelike pieces form. Combine the parsnip mixture, diced Wakame Salad, vinegar, honey, lemon juice, salt, and pepper in a bowl and mix well.

*To make the Carrot and Pea Tip Salad:* Combine all the ingredients in a bowl and mix well.

*To make the Wasabi Mayonnaise:* Combine the Pine Nut Mayonnaise, shoyu, wasabi, and lime juice in a bowl and stir to mix. Season to taste with salt and pepper. Set aside ¹/₄ cup to use for serving with the rolls. Reserve the remainder for another use.

*To form the sushi:* Place a nori sheet on a sushi mat. Spread one-fourth of the rice on the nori, leaving a ¹/₄-inch border at the bottom and sides and a 1-inch border at the top. Make a horizontal line across the middle of the rice with one-fourth each of the julienned avocado and daikon; the cucumber batons; the remaining Wakame Salad; the Carrot and Pea Tip Salad; and the daikon sprouts, allowing the sprouts to extend beyond one end. Using the sushi mat, roll up the nori into a firm sushi roll. Repeat with the remaining 3 nori sheets, rice, vegetables, and salads, to make 4 rolls in all. Trim the end without the daikon sprouts on each roll to even it neatly. Cut each sushi roll crosswise into 5 slices, making the slice with the daikon sprouts visible twice as thick as the others.

**Assembly**—Stand the sushi roll slices vertically on the center of each plate. Spoon one-fourth of the Wasabi Mayonnaise around the plate along with some of the liquid from the Wakame Salad. Drizzle 1 tablespoon of the shoyu around the plate and sprinkle with one-fourth of the chiffonade-cut nori.

**Wine Notes**—Austrian Grüner Veltliner is a crisp, mineral-style wine with notes of white pepper. Nikolaihof, a biodynamic wine maker, produces wines that reflect the individual vineyards in which their grapes were grown. Grüner is a compelling choice with this dish because of the mineral character of the root vegetables and the nori. Other elements of the dish are sparked with racy acidity, and this too is held in check by Austria's national grape.

**Serves 4**

### Wakame Salad

¹/₂ ounce dried wakame seaweed, soaked for 20 minutes in filtered water and drained

1 tablespoon brunoise-cut red bell pepper

2 tablespoons brunoise-cut pineapple

2 teaspoons chiffonade-cut fresh basil

¹/₄ cup nama shoyu

3 tablespoons rice wine vinegar

2 teaspoons cold-pressed sesame oil

### Sushi Rice

1 cup chopped, peeled parsnip

¹/₃ cup raw pine nuts

¹/₄ cup diced Wakame Salad

2 tablespoons rice wine vinegar

1 tablespoon raw honey

1 tablespoon freshly squeezed lemon juice

¹/₄ teaspoon Celtic sea salt

1 teaspoon freshly cracked pepper

### Carrot and Pea Tip Salad

¹/₂ cup julienned carrot

¹/₂ cup pea shoot tips

¹/₄ teaspoon extra virgin olive oil

¹/₈ teaspoon nama shoyu

¹/₈ teaspoon chopped nori

¹/₈ teaspoon freshly squeezed lemon juice

¹/₈ teaspoon coarsely crushed white sesame seeds

### Wasabi Mayonnaise

¹/₂ cup Pine Nut Mayonnaise (see Appendices)

¹/₄ teaspoon nama shoyu

¹/₂ teaspoon freshly grated wasabi

¹/₄ teaspoon freshly squeezed lime juice

Celtic sea salt and freshly ground pepper

4 sheets nori

¹/₂ avocado, peeled and julienned

¹/₂ cup julienned daikon

¹/₂ cucumber, skin on, cut into 1 by ¹/₄-inch batons

¹/₂ cup daikon sprouts

4 tablespoons nama shoyu

2 tablespoons fine-chiffonade-cut nori

## Three Peppercorn–Crusted Cashew Cheese with Honeycomb and Balsamic Vinegar

*This is a stunning combination of textures and flavors. First, there are the juxtapositions of the crunchy peppercorn pieces and the creamy cheese, the crispy Smoked Almonds and the chewy dried apricots, the erotic gooeyness of the honeycomb mounds and the elegant crispiness of the thyme sprouts. Then we have heat, sweetness, pepperiness, sourness, and acidity all rolled into one. The result is a complex, yet harmonious, enticement.*

**Method**—*To make the Smoked Almonds:* Drain the almonds, place in a bowl, and toss with the smoked salt. Spread the almonds on a nonstick drying sheet on a dehydrator shelf and dehydrate at 105°F for 24 hours, or until crisp. Remove the almonds from the dehydrator, quarter 4 almonds lengthwise, and coarsely chop 8 almonds. Reserve the remaining almonds for another use.

*To prepare the cheese:* Press the Cashew Cheese into a ring mold 5 inches in diameter and 1 inch deep. Combine all the peppercorns in a bowl, stir well, and then sprinkle the peppercorn mix onto the top of the cheese. Cover and refrigerate for 1 hour. Carefully remove the cheese from the mold and cut into 4 wedges.

**Assembly**—Place a wedge of the peppercorn-crusted cheese on each plate. Arrange one-fourth of the honeycomb pieces, dried apricots, and Smoked Almonds in a line down the plate. Spoon 1 teaspoon of the vinegar around the honeycomb pieces, apricots, and almonds. Sprinkle with 2 teaspoons of the thyme sprouts and salt to taste.

**Wine Notes**—Abundantly scented Chenin Blanc from the Loire Valley reflects the honey, apricot, and smoked almond flavors of the dish. The Cashew Cheese is generously crusted with peppercorns, which adds up to some spicy heat. Savennières made by Nicolas Joly is a unique and complex wine that becomes more focused when it is paired with this course. Joly is also one of the most outspoken champions of biodynamic farming.

**Serves 4**

**Smoked Almonds**

1 cup raw almonds, soaked for 8 to 10 hours in filtered water

1/4 teaspoon smoked salt, crushed

1 cup Cashew Cheese (see Appendices)

1 1/2 teaspoons black peppercorns, crushed

1 1/2 teaspoons green peppercorns, crushed

1 tablespoon pink peppercorn shells, crushed

1/4 pound honeycomb, broken into small pieces just before using

1/4 cup chopped dried apricots

4 teaspoons 12-year-old Villa Manodori balsamic vinegar

8 teaspoons micro thyme sprouts

Celtic sea salt

## Layered Morel Mushrooms and Fennel with Two Vinaigrettes: Opal Basil and Mustard Seed

*This preparation is simultaneously earthy and refined. The flavors of the morels and the fennel work together harmoniously, and both are successfully offset by the accompanying vinaigrettes. The opal basil in one provides a clean, peppery, floral flavor, while the mustard seeds and the chile vinegar in the other add a refreshing and decisive bite that nicely harnesses all the flavors on the plate.*

**Method**—*To make the Fennel Purée:* In a high-speed blender, combine the chopped fennel, 1 tablespoon water, and the olive oil and process until smooth and thick, adding more water if needed to create a thick, but not stiff, consistency. Season to taste with salt and pepper. Set aside about $3/4$ cup to use for the layering the morel slices. Reserve the remainder for another use.

*To prepare the morels:* Combine the morels, water, and olive oil in a bowl and let soak for 1 hour to rehydrate. Remove the morels from the liquid and slice each mushroom into $1/2$-inch-thick rings. (Save the trimmings for another use.)

*To prepare the sliced fennel:* Combine the sliced fennel, olive oil, and lemon juice in a bowl and toss to mix. Season to taste with salt and pepper.

*To make the Opal Basil Vinaigrette:* Whisk together the olive oil, vinegar, and basil in a bowl. Season to taste with salt and pepper.

*To make the Mustard Vinaigrette:* Whisk together the olive oil, vinegar, and mustard seeds in a bowl. Season to taste with salt and pepper.

**Assembly**—*To layer the morel slices:* Place a morel mushroom ring on a work surface and place a few marinated fennel slices on the ring. Spoon 2 teaspoons of the Fennel Purée over the slices and top with a fennel frond. Top with a second mushroom ring, followed by a few marinated fennel slices, and 2 more teaspoons Fennel Purée. Top with a final mushroom ring and then a fennel frond. Repeat until you have 8 mushrooms stacks in all.

Place 2 mushroom stacks in the center of each plate. Spoon the Opal Basil Vinaigrette and Mustard Vinaigrette around the mushroom stacks. Top with pepper.

**Wine Notes**—Morel mushrooms are a luxury food item, so why not pair them with a truly special bottle of wine? The feminine grace of Comte de Vogue's Musigny Vieilles Vignes makes it the quintessential Burgundy. The earthy, mushroomy, and anisey flavors of the dish call for a wine that has bottle age to soften its hard edges. Lighter-bodied Pinot Noir from the village of Chambolle-Musigny, where the grand cru Musigny Vineyard is found, not only tastes like the soil in which it was grown, but also has the elegance and finesse to allow all of the flavors in the dish to be appreciated.

**Serves 4**

**Fennel Purée**

1 cup chopped fennel

1 to 2 tablespoons filtered water

2 tablespoons extra virgin olive oil

Celtic sea salt and freshly ground pepper

**Morels**

12 large dried morel mushrooms

$1\,1/2$ cups filtered water

2 tablespoons extra virgin olive oil

**Sliced Fennel**

$1/3$ cup thinly sliced fennel

1 tablespoon extra virgin olive oil

2 teaspoons freshly squeezed lemon juice

Celtic sea salt and freshly ground pepper

**Opal Basil Vinaigrette**

$1/4$ cup extra virgin olive oil

1 tablespoon white wine vinegar

3 tablespoons finely chopped fresh opal basil

Celtic sea salt and freshly ground pepper

**Mustard Vinaigrette**

1 tablespoon extra virgin olive oil

2 tablespoons chile vinegar

2 tablespoons mustard seeds, soaked for 10 to 12 hours in filtered water and drained

Celtic sea salt and freshly ground pepper

16 fennel fronds, each 1 inch long

Freshly ground pepper

# Salsify with Black Truffles and Porcini Mushrooms

*Salsify and black truffles are great friends and always make for a rewarding combination. They gain an added elegance and depth here with the addition of porcini slices. A purée of pine nuts provides a heavenly texture that knits all the elements together. Truffle oil, flat-leaf parsley, and fleur de sel round out the dish.*

**Method**—*To prepare the salsify:* Combine the salsify, water, and vinegar in a bowl and let soak for 24 hours. Remove the salsify from the liquid, reserving the liquid. Using a vegetable peeler, peel the salsify into long ribbons. Return the salsify ribbons to the liquid and let soak for 2 hours.

*To prepare the fresh porcini:* Combine the mushrooms, vinegar, and olive oil in a bowl and toss to mix. Season to taste with salt and pepper.

*To make the Porcini Chips:* If you are unable to create slices that include both the cap and stem, cut a few extra cap slices. Arrange the slices on a nonstick drying sheet on a dehydrator shelf and dehydrate at 105°F for 4 to 6 hours, or until dry. Remove the slices from the sheet while they are still warm, using a spatula if necessary to loosen them.

*To make the Pine Nut Purée:* In a high-speed blender, combine the pine nuts, lemon juice, and $1/4$ cup water and process until smooth, adding the remaining 1 tablespoon water as needed to create a saucelike consistency. Season to taste with salt and pepper. (The lemon juice will make the sauce coagulate slightly.)

**Assembly**—Drain the salsify ribbons, place in a bowl, add 2 teaspoons of the truffle oil, and toss to coat the ribbons evenly. Season to taste with salt. Layer one-fourth of the salsify ribbons, fresh porcini mushrooms, truffle slices, and Porcini Chips in the center of each plate. Spoon one-fourth each of the Pine Nut Purée and of the remaining white truffle oil around the plate. Sprinkle with the fleur de sel to taste and 1 teaspoon of the parsley. Top with white pepper.

**Wine Notes**—Without a doubt, truffle is the dominant aroma of this preparation, and the chosen wine must not mask this heady flavor. Châteauneuf-du-Pape Blanc from Château Rayas would be a luxurious pairing, as would a Hermitage Blanc from Jean-Louis Chave. Both of these wines will allow the truffles to play the leading role, while they stand in the background and highlight the mineral nature of the porcini and salsify.

## Serves 4

### Salsify

3 thick stalks salsify, peeled

2 cups filtered water

$1/2$ cup white wine vinegar

### Fresh Porcini Mushrooms

$1 1/2$ cups thinly sliced porcini mushroom caps and stems

2 teaspoons white wine vinegar

1 tablespoon extra virgin olive oil

Celtic sea salt and freshly ground pepper

### Porcini Chips

12 thin porcini mushroom slices, including stem

### Pine Nut Purée

$1/2$ cup raw pine nuts, soaked for 8 to 10 hours in filtered water and drained

$1 1/2$ tablespoons freshly squeezed lemon juice

$1/4$ cup plus 1 tablespoon filtered water

Celtic sea salt and freshly ground pepper

2 tablespoons white truffle oil

Fleur de sel

1 black truffle, thinly sliced

4 teaspoons fresh flat-leaf parsley leaves, cut into chiffonade

Freshly ground white pepper

# Pear Napoleon with Porcini Mushrooms and Artichokes

*Although the flavor combination here is familiar, in this preparation the result is considerably more profound. The sweet Warren pears are presented both crispy (dehydrated) and fresh, the porcini slices are meaty yet refined, and the artichoke pieces deliver a delicate crunchiness. Additionally, the chopped cashews provide a lusty richness, while the shiso, thyme, and peppercorns round out the flavors beautifully. This is a dish that will satisfy virtually every palate.*

**Method**—*To prepare the artichokes:* Combine all the ingredients in a bowl, toss to mix, cover, and marinate in the refrigerator for 3 days. Remove the artichokes from the marinade and thinly slice them vertically. Reserve the marinade.

*To make the Pear Chips:* Lightly coat the pear slices with the lemon juice, and place on a nonstick drying sheet on a dehydrator shelf. Dehydrate at 105°F for 8 to 10 hours, or until crisp. Remove the chips from the sheet while they are still warm, using a spatula if necessary to loosen them. You will need only 12 chips for the recipe, but they are fragile and you may lose a few, so the 4 extra are insurance. Store the chips in an airtight container at room temperature until ready to use.

*To prepare the pears:* Combine the pears, olive oil, and salt in a bowl and toss together vigorously. This will slightly mash the pears and help to release their sweet juices into the olive oil.

*To prepare the mushrooms:* Combine the mushrooms and olive oil in a bowl and toss to coat. Season to taste with salt and pepper.

**Assembly**—In the center of each plate, make a layer of porcini mushroom slices. Top with artichoke slices, pear pieces, and a Pear Chip. Repeat the layering twice, until you have 3 layers of filling and 3 layers of Pear Chips. Spoon the remaining pear pieces and the juices from their bowl around the plate. Arrange a few of the shallot rings, the peppercorns, and the Spicy Cashews around the plate. Sprinkle with the thyme sprigs and the orach and shiso sprouts. Top with pepper.

**Wine Notes**—Artichokes always make a sommelier sweat. In this preparation, they are cleverly combined with pears and porcini. Englegarten, a field blend by Marcel Deiss, is about 90 percent Riesling, with the remainder split between Muscat and Pinot Gris. The wine balances the use of vinegar in the dish and tempers the heat from the chili powder–dusted cashews.

**Serves 4**

### Artichokes

3 baby artichoke bottoms or 1 regular-sized artichoke bottom, choke and stem removed

$1/4$ cup Cabernet Sauvignon wine vinegar

1 rosemary sprig, broken into 3 pieces

3 thyme sprigs

1 teaspoon peppercorns

2 cloves garlic, smashed

1 small shallot, thinly sliced into rings

$1/4$ cup extra virgin olive oil

### Pear Chips

2 Warren pears, skin on, halved, cored, and cut lengthwise into a minimum of 16 slices, each $1/16$ inch thick

2 teaspoons freshly squeezed lemon juice

### Pears

2 ripe Warren pears, preferably from Frog Hollow Farm, peeled, halved, cored, and cut into small wedges

$1 1/2$ tablespoons olive oil

Pinch of Celtic sea salt

### Porcini Mushrooms

2 porcini mushroom caps, sliced $1/8$ inch thick

2 teaspoons extra virgin olive oil

Celtic sea salt and freshly ground pepper

### Garnish

Shallot rings from artichoke marinade

Peppercorns from artichoke marinade

2 tablespoons chopped Spicy Cashews (see Appendices)

Thyme sprigs from artichoke marinade, broken into 1-inch pieces

2 tablespoons micro red orach sprouts

2 tablespoons micro green shiso sprouts

Freshly ground pepper

# Daikon Lo Mein

*Paper-thin daikon slices emulate delicate, toothsome noodles, while the beans and herbs add crunchiness. A purée that includes peppery watercress and Mexican tarragon conveys an exciting zestiness, and a scattering of tangy wolfberries rounds out the dish with a subtle opulence. The final element of brilliant flavor comes from fine strands of chile, which contribute just the right riveting accent. This preparation is guaranteed to startle and seduce even the most experienced palate.*

**Method**—Using a vegetable peeler, peel the daikon. Cut the daikon in half lengthwise, then cut each half lengthwise into 3/4-inch-thick strips. Again using the peeler, cut the daikon into paper-thin strips about 1 inch wide and 4 inches long. Place the strips in a bowl, add the lime juice and salt and pepper to taste, and toss to mix.

Combine the romano beans, vinegar, and sesame oil in a bowl and toss to mix. Season to taste with salt and pepper.

*To make the Herb Sauce:* In a high-speed blender, combine the spinach, tarragon, watercress, garlic, water, and olive oil and process until smooth. Season to taste with salt and pepper.

**Assembly**—Spoon a ring of the Herb Sauce in an oval on each plate. Arrange one-fourth of the daikon strips, romano bean salad, wolfberries, and red and orange chile pieces in the center of the sauce. Sprinkle with the cilantro sprouts and scallions, and drizzle some of the water from the wolfberries around the sauce.

**Wine Notes**—The heat factor in this dish is high. A dry wine and/or one with high alcohol will only exacerbate this spiciness. Pfeffingen's Scheurebe Spätlese from the Pfalz region of Germany has the balance of residual sugar and acid necessary to integrate with the dish. The wine's tropical fruit flavors offer a marked contrast to the strong tarragon and herb flavors.

## Serves 4

1 4-inch piece daikon

Juice of 1/2 medium lime

Celtic sea salt and freshly ground pepper

8 green romano beans, thinly cut on the diagonal

1/2 teaspoon red wine vinegar

1 tablespoon cold-pressed sesame oil

### Herb Sauce

1 cup firmly packed spinach leaves

1/2 cup firmly packed fresh Mexican tarragon leaves

1 cup young, tender watercress leaves with stems

1 clove garlic

6 tablespoons filtered water

4 teaspoons extra virgin olive oil

Celtic sea salt and freshly ground pepper

### Garnish

1/4 cup dried wolfberries, soaked for 5 hours in filtered water, drained, and water reserved

1 red Thai chile, seeded and very finely julienned

1 orange Thai chile, seeded and very finely julienned

1/4 cup micro cilantro sprouts

2 scallions, white part only, thinly cut on the diagonal

# Open-Faced Cheese and Tomato Tart

*The flavors and textures of this dish draw on the Mediterranean pantry. Tomatoes, both raw and dehydrated, burst with flavor and provide the perfect sweet-acid balance to counter the lusty cheese and the rich-tasting tart. Basil and spinach also assert their personalities and round out the other flavors superbly. A bonus: this tart works as an appetizer or a main course.*

**Method**—Combine the tomato slices, olive oil, and basil in a bowl and toss to mix. Season to taste with salt and pepper. Arrange the tomato slices on a dehydrator shelf and dehydrate at 105°F for 8 hours, or until dry. Julienne 4 pieces and reserve the whole slices and julienned pieces separately.

*To make the tart bases:* In a food processor, combine all the ingredients, using only 1 1/2 teaspoons water if the zucchini is very watery, and process until the ingredients come together in a ball. There will be small particles of the zucchini visible. Wrap the ball in plastic wrap and refrigerate for 20 minutes.

Remove the ball from the refrigerator, flatten into a disk, and place between 2 nonstick drying sheets. Using a rolling pin, roll out 1/8 inch thick. Using a 3-inch round cookie or biscuit cutter, cut out 4 rounds. Gather up the scraps and make 4 balls of 1 tablespoon each. Roll out each ball into a rope long enough to fit completely around the edge of a round, then place each rope on a round, creating an attractive rim. Press down so the rope adheres to the rim. Place the tart bases on a dehydrator shelf and dehydrate at 105°F for 2 hours, or until dry. Refrigerate until needed.

*To make the Cheese Filling:* Combine the cheese, spinach, and rosemary in a bowl and mix well. Season to taste with salt and pepper.

*To make the Basil Vinaigrette:* Combine the garlic, lemon zest, basil, and olive oil in a mortar and grind together with a pestle until all the elements are fully incorporated. Season to taste with salt.

Combine the green zebra tomato wedges and the arugula in a bowl, drizzle with the olive oil, and toss to coat evenly. Season to taste with salt and pepper.

**Assembly**—Spread 3 tablespoons of the Cheese Filling in the bottom of each tart base. Arrange one-fourth of the tomatoes and arugula mixture and 3 dehydrated tomato slices over the filling on each tart. Spoon one-fourth of the Basil Vinaigrette around the plate and sprinkle one-fourth of the julienned tomato on the vinaigrette. Top with pepper.

**Wine Notes**—The green notes, as well as the tomatoes, work well with Sauvignon Blanc, but the Cashew Cheese overwhelms a lean, mineral Sancerre. A fuller-bodied, fruit-forward Sauvignon Blanc from California is the answer. Duckhorn's Sauvignon Blanc can stand up to the cheese, and has enough brightness to complement the other flavors.

**Serves 4**

16 red tomato slices, each 1/3 inch thick, peeled

2 tablespoons extra virgin olive oil

2 teaspoons chopped fresh basil

Celtic sea salt and freshly ground pepper

**Tart Bases**

1/2 cup Almond Flour (see Appendices)

1/4 cup golden flax meal

1/4 cup chopped, peeled zucchini

2 tablespoons raw almond butter

1 tablespoon minced yellow onion

1 1/2 to 3 teaspoons filtered water

1/4 teaspoon Celtic sea salt

**Cheese Filling**

1/2 cup Cashew Cheese (see Appendices)

1/4 cup chopped spinach leaves

1 teaspoon finely chopped fresh rosemary

Celtic sea salt and freshly ground pepper

**Basil Vinaigrette**

1 small clove garlic, minced

1 tablespoon grated lemon zest

1/4 cup chopped fresh basil

1/4 cup extra virgin olive oil

Celtic sea salt

4 green zebra tomatoes, each cut into 8 wedges

2 cups baby arugula

2 tablespoons extra virgin olive oil

Celtic sea salt and freshly ground pepper

# Mung Bean Salad Wrapped in Swiss Chard with Marinated Vegetables and Thai Vinaigrette

The flavors in this preparation just go and go. The Thai Vinaigrette with its focused and elegant heat stitches together the disparate components with a masterful weave. While the mung bean sprouts are definitely the star of the filling, the water chestnuts, Thai basil, and celery leaves are extraordinary contributions. Nor can the supporting cast of marinated cucumbers and the ultra-exotic cauliflower mushrooms be overlooked. Best of all though may be the variety of textures experienced on the palate when the dish is consumed. Indeed, fireworks go off!

**Method**—*To make the Swiss Chard Wrap:* In a food processor, combine the water chestnuts and 1 tablespoon water and process until smooth, adding more water as needed to create a thick purée. Pour into a bowl, add the bean sprouts, celery leaves, basil, chile, and sesame oil, and stir to mix. Season to taste with salt and pepper.

Lay the Swiss chard leaves, rib side up, on a work surface. Place one-fourth of the bean sprout mixture near the stem end of each leaf and roll up like a cigar. Trim and discard the ends.

*To prepare the cucumber:* Combine the cucumber and lime juice and toss to mix. Season to taste with salt. Cover and refrigerate for 2 hours before serving.

*To prepare the cauliflower mushrooms:* Combine the mushrooms, citron juice, vinegar, and chile and toss to coat evenly. Season to taste with salt.

*To make the Thai Vinaigrette:* Combine the shoyu, lime juice, Swiss chard, chile, and coriander in a bowl and stir to mix. Season to taste with salt.

**Assembly**—Place a Swiss Chard Wrap in the center of each plate, positioning it at a slight angle. Arrange 3 mounds of the cauliflower mushrooms at 10 o'clock, 11 o'clock, and 3 o'clock. Place the cucumber at 9 o'clock. Drizzle the Thai Vinaigrette around the plate and sprinkle with the basil leaves.

**Wine Notes**—Lime juice and the herbal notes from the Thai basil and the Swiss chard call for a high-acid Sauvignon Blanc. Terrunyo from Concha y Toro is a single-vineyard Sauvignon Blanc from Chile's Casablanca Valley. Packed with citrus aromas and racy acidity, it has just the flavors to elevate this course to another level.

## Serves 4

### Swiss Chard Wrap

6 water chestnuts, peeled and chopped

1 to 2 tablespoons filtered water

1/2 cup loosely packed mung bean sprouts, "tails" removed

2 tablespoons loosely packed celery leaves, chopped

1 tablespoon loosely packed fresh Thai basil leaves, cut into chiffonade

1 red Thai chile, seeded and minced

2 tablespoons cold-pressed sesame oil

Celtic sea salt and freshly ground pepper

4 small Swiss chard leaves, stems removed

### Marinated Cucumber

1 cup thinly sliced cucumber, skin on

Juice of 1 lime, strained

Celtic sea salt

### Dried Cauliflower Mushrooms

1 cup dried cauliflower mushrooms, soaked for 2 hours in filtered water and drained

1/4 cup yuzu citron juice

1 tablespoon rice wine vinegar

1/2 red Thai chile, seeded and thinly sliced on the diagonal

Celtic sea salt

### Thai Vinaigrette

1/4 cup nama shoyu

1 tablespoon freshly squeezed lime juice

1 3-inch piece Swiss chard leaf, cut into fine chiffonade

1 red Thai chile, thinly sliced on the diagonal

1 teaspoon freshly coarse-ground coriander

Celtic sea salt

2 teaspoons fresh micro basil leaves

# Cucumber Summer Rolls

*These incredibly refreshing Summer Rolls work wonderfully either as plated appetizers or passed hors d'oeuvres. Cilantro and young coconut are packaged neatly in razor-thin slices of cucumber. The overall result, while seemingly rich, literally disappears in your mouth. The leftover marinade and a little sesame oil sparsely drizzled about the plate add the final flavor notes.*

**Method**—*To make the marinade:* Combine the shoyu, lemon juice, ginger, garlic, chile, and maple syrup in a bowl and whisk to mix. Season to taste with pepper.

*To make the Summer Rolls:* Cut each cucumber crosswise into three 4-inch-long logs. Using a mandoline, cut the cucumber logs lengthwise into a total of 48 paper-thin slices. Lay 4 of the slices side by side, overlapping them slightly, to form a 6-inch square. Repeat to make 12 squares in all.

Combine the avocado, carrot, bell pepper, coconut meat, lettuce, ginger, cilantro, cold-pressed sesame oil, and $1/4$ cup of the marinade in a bowl and toss to mix. Season to taste with salt and pepper.

Working with 1 cucumber square at a time, lay it on a flat work surface. Spoon one-twelfth of the vegetable mixture along the bottom third of the square. Arrange some of the daikon sprouts at one end of the vegetable mixture. Roll up the square tightly, enclosing the vegetable mixture and keeping the sprouts visible at the end. Repeat to make 12 rolls in all. Cut 4 of the cucumber rolls in half.

**Assembly**—Lay 2 Summer Rolls in the center of each plate, and arrange the 2 halves of one of the cut rolls to one side. Spoon the remaining marinade and the chile-infused sesame oil around and over the rolls. Sprinkle with the celery sprouts and top with pepper.

**Wine Notes**—The amount of spiciness, or heat, in this dish directs the wine choice. The chiles and ginger overpower dry Alsatian Rieslings, while their counterparts in Mosel-Saar-Ruwer have enough sweetness to hold the spices in check. Spätlese Rieslings from Fritz Haag are light in body, preventing them from overwhelming the course. Haag's wines never touch new oak, and this steeliness highlights the earthy, mineral flavors of the cucumbers and other vegetables.

**Serves 4**

### Marinade

$1/2$ cup white shoyu

2 tablespoons plus 2 teaspoons freshly squeezed lemon juice

2 tablespoons minced, peeled fresh ginger

1 clove garlic, minced

1 red Thai chile, seeded and minced

2 teaspoons maple syrup

Freshly ground pepper

### Summer Rolls

2 English cucumbers, each at least 12 inches long, peeled

$1/2$ avocado, peeled and julienned

$1/2$ carrot, 3 to 4 inches long, peeled and julienned

1 small red bell pepper, seeded and julienned

1 small young Thai coconut, meat julienned

1 cup red oak-leaf lettuce, torn into tiny pieces

2 tablespoons finely julienned, peeled fresh ginger

2 tablespoons fresh cilantro leaves, torn

1 tablespoon cold-pressed sesame oil

Celtic sea salt and freshly ground pepper

$1/2$ cup daikon sprouts

### Garnish

1 tablespoon chile-infused cold-pressed sesame oil

2 tablespoons micro celery sprouts

Freshly ground pepper

# Tengusa Seaweed Gelée with Sea Beans and Jalapeño-Lemongrass Vinaigrette

*A crisp mixture of sea beans, celery leaves, and tiny pieces of tengusa seaweed is wrapped in thin sheets of seaweed gelée. Once the Jalapeño-Lemongrass Vinaigrette is spooned over the top, the combination comes alive with distinctive flavors.*

**Method**—*To make the Tengusa Seaweed Gelée:* Place the seaweed in a shallow bowl and pour the hot water over it. Let stand for 1 hour to rehydrate. Remove the seaweed from the water, measure out $1/2$ cup seaweed, and set it aside. Measure 3 cups of the soaking water and discard the remainder. In a high-speed blender, combine the 3 cups soaking water, the remaining seaweed, and the agar-agar and process until smooth. Mix in the shoyu and lemon juice and season to taste with salt and pepper.

Line a jelly-roll pan with plastic wrap, allowing it to overhang the edges by a few inches. Pour the tengusa gelée mixture into the pan and spread it into a smooth layer $1/4$ inch thick. Refrigerate for 12 hours, or until firm. Remove the pan from the refrigerator and invert it onto a cutting board. Lift off the pan and peel away the plastic wrap. Trim away any ragged edges and cut the gelée into 12 pieces, each 3 by 4 inches. Line the pan with a fresh sheet of plastic wrap, return the gelée pieces to the pan, and return to the refrigerator until needed.

*To make the filling:* Combine the sea beans, celery leaves, lemon pieces, and half of the reserved tengusa seaweed in a bowl and stir to mix. Season to taste with salt.

*To make the Jalapeño-Lemongrass Vinaigrette:* Whisk together the chile, cherry peppers, lemongrass, olive oil, and lemon juice in a bowl. Season to taste with salt.

*To make the garnish:* Cut the nori into a fine brunoise and toss with the citron juice and shoyu. Reserve the lemongrass and lemon zest.

**Assembly**—Lay the tengusa seaweed pieces on a flat work surface, with the long sides facing you. Place an equal amount of the filling horizontally at the base of each piece, extending the ends of the sea beans beyond the edges of the piece. Starting at the long side nearest you, tightly roll up each gelée piece into a cigar shape.

Place 3 gelée rolls in the center of each plate. Spoon one-fourth of the Suizenji nori and the vinaigrette evenly over the rolls. Sprinkle with the remaining tengusa seaweed pieces, the lemongrass, and the lemon zest.

**Wine Notes**—The prominent flavors of this dish are the sea beans and the tengusa seaweed, with the lemongrass also adding an interesting note. Maysara Pinot Gris from Oregon produces a fascinating pairing. It delivers enough minerality to complement the two seaweeds and has a touch of sweetness that tones down the jalapeño in the vinaigrette.

## Serves 4

### Tengusa Seaweed Gelée

6 ounces dried tengusa seaweed

4 cups hot (118°F) filtered water

$1/4$ cup powdered agar-agar, dissolved in $1/2$ cup hot (118°F) filtered water

3 tablespoons nama shoyu

2 teaspoons freshly squeezed lemon juice

Celtic sea salt and freshly ground pepper

### Filling

$3/4$ pound sea beans

$1/4$ cup celery leaves, coarsely chopped

1 Meyer lemon, supremed and each segment cut into 4 pieces

Celtic sea salt

### Jalapeño-Lemongrass Vinaigrette

1 jalapeño chile, seeded and minced

2 orange cherry peppers, halved, seeded, and cut lengthwise into thin strands

2 teaspoons finely shaved lemongrass

$1/4$ cup extra virgin olive oil

$1 1/2$ tablespoons freshly squeezed lemon juice

Celtic sea salt

### Garnish

4 ounces dried Suizenji nori, soaked for 1 hour in tepid filtered water and drained

2 tablespoons yuzu citron juice

2 tablespoons nama shoyu

1 teaspoon finely shaved lemongrass

Finely grated zest of 1 lemon, removed with a Microplane grater

# Broccoflower Couscous with Curry Oil and Aged Balsamic Vinegar

*This preparation is inspired by a similar idea from genius chef Ferran Adrià of Spain. The broccoflower is finely cut to emulate the look of couscous. Here, though, champagne grapes have been added to provide a burst of sweet fruit juice. Also present are accents of curry and aged balsamic vinegar, both of which lend a poignant and exotic note, making for an overall stunning complexity of flavor. Wisps of herbs complete this intoxicating dish.*

**Method**—*To make the couscous:* Combine the broccoflower, grapes, carrot, parsley, tarragon, cilantro, lavender, coriander, olive oil, champagne vinegar, and orange juice in a bowl and stir to mix. Season to taste with salt and pepper.

**Assembly**—Place a shallow ring mold 5 inches in diameter in the center of each plate. Fill it to a depth of $1/2$ inch with the couscous, and then gently press on the couscous with the back of a spoon. Remove the ring mold. Drizzle 1 teaspoon of the Curry Oil and 1 teaspoon of the vinegar around the plate, and sprinkle with the chervil, tarragon, and parsley leaves.

**Wine Notes**—One of the classic pairings with curry is Gewürztraminer, and this is no exception. Use caution and do not overpower the tender grape and broccoflower flavors with an excessively ripe and sweet wine. Going with a leaner producer such as Trimbach or Lorentz from Alsace is a preferable choice. A New World Gewürztraminer from Edmeades in California's Anderson Valley also matches the spiciness of the curry and the hint of sweetness from the balsamic vinegar.

## Serves 4

### Couscous

$1/2$ head broccoflower, broken into florets the size of tiny peas

1 cup champagne grapes, stems removed

$1/3$ cup fine-brunoise-cut carrot

2 tablespoons chopped fresh flat-leaf parsley

1 tablespoon chopped fresh tarragon

1 tablespoon chopped fresh cilantro

1 teaspoon fresh lavender, soaked for 15 minutes in filtered water, drained, patted dry, and lightly crushed

$1\,1/2$ teaspoons freshly ground coriander seeds

$1/4$ cup extra virgin olive oil

2 tablespoons champagne vinegar

2 tablespoons freshly squeezed orange juice

Celtic sea salt and freshly ground pepper

### Garnish

4 teaspoons Curry Oil (see Appendices)

4 teaspoons 25-year-old Villa Manodori balsamic vinegar

1 tablespoon fresh chervil leaves

2 teaspoons fresh tiny tarragon leaves

2 teaspoons fresh micro flat-leaf parsley leaves

SOUPS

# Shiitake Mushroom Soup with Lime Radish and Winged Beans

*Here is a study in exquisite texture. Lightly crunchy slices of radish and winged bean dance on the tongue. Shiitake mushroom pieces counter with just the right toothsomeness. The result is an ethereal preparation that champions simple and profound flavors simultaneously. Additional mushrooms can be added for a more substantial course.*

**Method**—*To make the soup:* Drain the mushrooms in a sieve placed over a bowl, and reserve the mushrooms and water separately. Season the reserved water with the shoyu. Discard the stems from the mushrooms and julienne the caps. Set aside 3/4 cup to use with the soup. You will have extra mushrooms; save them for another use.

*To prepare the lime radish:* Combine all the ingredients in a bowl and toss to mix. Marinate for 30 minutes. Drain the radish slices in a sieve placed over a bowl, and reserve the radish slices and marinade separately.

**Assembly**—Add the reserved radish marinade to the mushroom liquid, and season to taste with salt, if needed. Ladle one-fourth of the mixture into each shallow bowl. Arrange one-fourth of the lime radish slices, one-fourth of the shiitake mushroom slices, 4 of the garlic shoot tops, and one-fourth of the chayote, red radishes, and winged beans in the bowl.

**Wine Notes**—These are *wine* notes in a *raw* book, but this dish is best paired with beer or, perhaps even better, left unaccompanied. The mushroom broth was entirely disjointed with every wine tasted, but found a loving companion with Sapporo beer. Rather than masking the broth's flavor, as all of the wines did, the Sapporo boosted it without dominating the radish or the garlic shoots.

**Serves 4**

**Soup**

3 cups dried shiitake mushrooms, soaked for 3 hours in 6 cups filtered water

3 tablespoons nama shoyu

**Lime Radish**

12 paper-thin slices lime radish

2 tablespoons white shoyu

1 tablespoon rice wine vinegar

2 teaspoons freshly squeezed Meyer lemon juice

Celtic sea salt, if needed

16 garlic shoots, tops cut off and reserved

1/2 cup very thinly sliced, peeled chayote

4 red radishes, sliced paper-thin

6 winged beans, sliced paper-thin on the diagonal

# Heirloom Tomato Soup with Arbequina Olives and Shaved Fennel

*Although this soup has a robust tomato flavor, it is surprisingly satiny and creamy, a result achieved by blending cucumber into the tomatoes. Chopped jalapeño provides a refreshing bite, shaved fennel adds crunch, and arbequina olives contribute both earthiness and meatiness. A final drizzle of olive oil is all that is needed to push this splendid dish over the top.*

**Method**—*To make the soup:* In a high-speed blender, combine the tomatoes, chile, cucumber, and vinegar and process until smooth. Pass the purée through a fine-mesh sieve and season to taste with salt and pepper.

**Assembly**—Ladle one-fourth of the soup into each bowl. Garnish with the fennel, olives, and tomato. Drizzle the olive brine, vinegar, and olive oil around the soup. Sprinkle with the fennel sprouts.

**Wine Notes**—The flavors of this dish are reminiscent of Provence, making a rosé possible. A Bandol Rosé from Domaine Tempier would be a serious selection with a complexity that other rosés often lack. This choice would accentuate the tomatoes and olive elements. An alternative would be to look to Albarino, a high-acid, aromatic varietal usually found in northwestern Spain. Napa Valley's Havens Wine Cellars makes an Albarino from Carneros, an option that will also excite the palate.

**Serves 4**

**Soup**

2 large, red heirloom tomatoes, peeled and seeded

$1/2$ jalapeño chile, seeded and chopped

$1/2$ cup chopped, peeled cucumber

2 teaspoons sherry wine vinegar

Celtic sea salt and freshly ground pepper

**Garnish**

1 3-inch-long baby fennel, thinly shaved on a mandoline

12 arbequina olives, pitted and quartered

$1/4$ cup peeled, seeded, and diced red tomato

2 teaspoons brine from olives

2 teaspoons sherry wine vinegar

1 tablespoon extra virgin olive oil

12 micro fennel sprouts or fennel fronds

# Cauliflower Soup with Balsamic Red Onions and Wilted Lettuce

*The ultrafine cauliflower purée makes the soup seem as if it is cream based — it's that shockingly satiny. The initial taste of the cauliflower comes off as earthy, but within moments it is clear just how regal this vegetable truly is. Dehydrated red onion pieces and Bibb lettuce leaves provide sweet and sharp flavor notes and a textural counterpoint, while a whisper of balsamic vinegar pushes this humble combination of ingredients to scale great heights.*

**Method**—*To make the soup:* In a high-speed blender, combine the cauliflower, olive oil, vinegar, and water and process until smooth and a thick saucelike consistency forms. Pass the soup though a medium-mesh sieve and season to taste with salt and pepper.

*To make the Balsamic Red Onions:* Use only the center onion slices; they should be at least 2 inches in diameter. Reserve the remaining slices for another use. Separate the slices into rings. Combine the onion, vinegar, and olive oil in a bowl and toss to mix. Season to taste with salt and pepper. Marinate at room temperature for 2 hours. Remove the onion rings from the bowl with a slotted spoon and place them in a single layer on a nonstick drying sheet on a dehydrator shelf. Reserve any marinating juices for garnish. Dehydrate at 105°F for 2 1/2 hours, or until tender and still slightly moist.

*To prepare the lettuce:* Combine the lettuce, vinegar, and olive oil in a bowl and toss to mix. Season to taste with salt and pepper. Transfer the lettuce to a sieve to drain. Arrange the lettuce in a single layer on a dehydrator shelf and dehydrate at 105°F for 30 minutes, or until wilted but not dried. Season to taste with salt and pepper.

**Assembly**—Ladle one-fourth of the soup into each bowl. Arrange some of the lettuce pieces and red onion slices around the bowl. Spoon some of the reserved onion marinating juices around the onion and lettuce.

**Wine Notes**—The soup is accented by the sweet-and-sour flavors of the balsamic onions. Oregon Pinot Gris from Sokol Blosser tames these flavors and has enough body to withstand the concentration in the soup. The wine delivers both a hint of sweetness and green, leafy notes to complement the wilted Bibb lettuce.

**Serves 4**

**Soup**

3 cups chopped cauliflower

1/4 cup extra virgin olive oil

2 tablespoons red wine vinegar

1 1/4 cups filtered water

Celtic sea salt and freshly ground pepper

**Balsamic Red Onions**

1 small red onion, sliced crosswise 1/8 inch thick

1/4 cup Villa Manodori balsamic vinegar

1 1/2 tablespoons extra virgin olive oil

Celtic sea salt and freshly ground pepper

**Lettuce**

8 Bibb lettuce leaves, torn into 2-inch pieces

1 tablespoon Villa Manodori balsamic vinegar

2 teaspoons extra virgin olive oil

Celtic sea salt and freshly ground pepper

# Butternut Squash and Ginger Soup with Spaghetti Squash

*The flavor of butternut squash explodes in your mouth the moment you sip this ultrasmooth soup. The butternut's natural sweetness is balanced by the ginger's pronounced assertiveness. Pieces of crispy butternut squash and shreds of softer spaghetti squash deliver a desirable contrast in texture, while thin slices of chile and wisps of tiny herbs provide a wonderful playfulness.*

**Method**—*To make the soup:* Arrange the 1 pound chopped butternut squash on a dehydrator shelf and dehydrate at 105°F for 18 hours, or until dry. Meanwhile, in a heavy-duty juicer, juice 2 cups of the chopped butternut squash. Discard the pulp and measure out $1/2$ cup juice.

In a high-speed blender, combine the dried squash, water, squash juice, the remaining $1/4$ cup chopped fresh squash, ginger, honey, and vinegar and process until smooth. Pass the purée through a fine-mesh sieve and season to taste with salt and pepper.

*To make the tuiles:* In a high-speed blender, combine the butternut squash, water, and olive oil and process until smooth. Put the purée in a fine-mesh sieve placed over a bowl and leave to drain for 15 minutes to remove excess liquid. Discard the liquid. Pass the purée through the same sieve and season to taste with salt and pepper.

Using a small offset spatula, make at least twelve $2 1/2$-inch rounds on nonstick drying sheets, spreading the purée thinly. (You will need 12 rounds for the recipe, but because they are fragile, making a few extra is a good idea.) Place the sheets on dehydrator shelves and dehydrate at 105°F for 4 to 6 hours, or until dry. Carefully peel the rounds from the sheet while they are still warm. Let cool completely, then store in an airtight container until ready to use. They will keep for up to 3 days.

*To prepare the spaghetti squash:* Using a fork, pull the drained shreds of squash into strands. Combine the squash, olive oil, vinegar, and scallion in a bowl and toss to mix. Season to taste with salt and pepper.

**Assembly**—Just before serving, assemble the squash tuiles: Place some of the spaghetti squash mixture on a tuile, top with a second tuile, spread it with some of the spaghetti squash mixture, and top with a third tuile. Repeat to make 4 layered squash tuiles in all. Ladle one-fourth of the soup into each shallow bowl, and lay 1 layered squash tuile on its side in the center of the soup. Sprinkle 1 teaspoon of the parsley and one-fourth of the Thai and banana chile slices on the surface of the soup, then drizzle with 1 teaspoon Herb Oil.

**Wine Notes**—Chiles and ginger deliver the spicy kick here. A Riesling Auslese from the Rheingau is a perfect counterpoint to the heat. Balthasar Ress produces outstanding wines from the Rudesheimer Berg Rottland, and these mate extremely well with the soup. The spaghetti squash adds an earthy, mineral element, which the Riesling also accents.

**Serves 4**

**Soup**

1 pound butternut squash, peeled, seeded, and chopped

$2 1/4$ cups chopped, peeled butternut squash

$1 3/4$ cups filtered water

2 tablespoons chopped, peeled fresh ginger

1 tablespoon raw clover honey

1 tablespoon sherry wine vinegar

Celtic sea salt and freshly ground pepper

**Tuiles**

1 cup chopped, peeled butternut squash

$1/2$ cup filtered water

3 tablespoons extra virgin olive oil

Celtic sea salt and freshly ground pepper

**Spaghetti Squash**

2 cups shredded, peeled very ripe spaghetti squash, soaked for 2 hours in filtered water and drained

$1 1/2$ tablespoons extra virgin olive oil

2 teaspoons white wine vinegar

2 tablespoons chopped scallion, green part only

Celtic sea salt and freshly ground pepper

**Garnish**

4 teaspoons fresh micro flat-leaf parsley leaves

2 red Thai chiles, thinly sliced

1 banana chile, thinly sliced

4 teaspoons Herb Oil (see Appendices)

## English Cucumber Soup with Tiny Carrots and Amaranth Leaves with Pine Nut Mayonnaise

*This dish is easy to make, but the result is stunningly complex on the palate. The soup is nothing more than a purée of English cucumber tinged with lemon juice and coarse sea salt. A playful salad of small carrots, cucumber pieces, scallion slices, and amaranth leaves adds textural contrast and substance. Finally, a drizzle of Pine Nut Mayonnaise and the olive oil provide a glorious richness. Ultimately, the flavors come across as simultaneously refreshing and haunting.*

**Method**—*To make the soup:* Just prior to serving, in a high-speed blender, process the cucumbers until smooth. Add the lemon juice and season to taste with salt and pepper.

*To make the Carrot Salad:* Just prior to serving, combine the carrots, scallion, cucumber, amaranth, olive oil, and lemon juice and toss to mix. Season to taste with salt and pepper.

**Assembly**—Arrange one-fourth of the Carrot Salad in the center of each bowl. Ladle one-fourth of the soup around the salad. Drizzle 1 teaspoon of the olive oil and 2 teaspoons of the Pine Nut Mayonnaise in a ring around the salad, then sprinkle the tarragon around the salad. Top with pepper.

**Wine Notes**—The cucumber soup has a briny, mineral character that is reminiscent of oysters and other shellfish. Given the delicate flavors of the soup and the restrained use of tarragon, a light-bodied Loire Valley wine from the Nantais is ideal. A Muscadet de Sèvre-et-Maine is not only a classic pairing for oysters, but also offers a seamless match with this course. Sauvion and Château de la Mouchetière have excellent examples.

---

Serves 4

**Soup**

2 English cucumbers, peeled and chopped

2 tablespoons freshly squeezed lemon juice

Celtic sea salt and freshly ground pepper

**Carrot Salad**

2 baby white carrots, peeled and sliced on the extreme diagonal

2 baby orange carrots, peeled and sliced on the extreme diagonal

2 baby red carrots, unpeeled and sliced on the extreme diagonal

1 tablespoon thinly sliced scallion, white and green parts, cut on the extreme diagonal

8 thin slices English cucumber, quartered

1/4 cup micro amaranth leaves

1 tablespoon extra virgin olive oil

1 teaspoon freshly squeezed lemon juice

Celtic sea salt and freshly ground pepper

**Garnish**

4 teaspoons extra virgin olive oil

8 teaspoons Pine Nut Mayonnaise (see Appendices)

1 tablespoon fresh micro tarragon leaves

Freshly ground pepper

## Red Bell Pepper Soup with Mango and Meyer Lemon

*This soup is light and refreshing but explosive in flavor. The clean heat of the horseradish tempers the natural sweetness of the bell pepper to help create just the right balance. Dabs of thickened Mango Purée add an exotic creaminess, and Meyer lemon pieces contribute a needed acidity. Finally, a fanciful touch comes in the form of fennel fronds and a grind of pepper. These generally familiar flavors will intrigue the palate in a new and provocative way.*

**Method**—*To make the soup:* In a heavy-duty juicer, juice the bell peppers. Discard the pulp and measure out 4 cups juice. Combine the bell pepper juice and horseradish juice in a bowl and stir to mix. Season to taste with salt and pepper. Taste and add the maple syrup if needed to sweeten.

*To make the Mango Purée:* In a high-speed blender, combine all the ingredients and process until smooth. Pour into a bowl, cover, and refrigerate for 1 hour, or until slightly firm.

**Assembly**—Ladle one-fourth of the soup into each bowl. Place 11 small dollops of the Mango Purée and one-fourth of the lemon segments around the soup. Sprinkle with the fennel fronds and top with pepper.

**Wine Notes**—The Butcher, a Zweigelt rosé from Schwarz, has all of the answers for this soup. A spicy kick from the horseradish juice is moderated by the sweetness of this Auslese, and the wine's high acid is the perfect foil for the Meyer lemon. This rosé also mirrors the fruitiness in the red bell pepper.

**Serves 4**

**Soup**

8 red bell peppers, seeded

1 tablespoon horseradish juice

Celtic sea salt and freshly ground pepper

1 teaspoon maple syrup, if needed

**Mango Purée**

1 mango, peeled, pitted, and chopped

2 tablespoons extra virgin olive oil

$1/4$ teaspoon powdered agar-agar

1 teaspoon Celtic sea salt

**Garnish**

12 Meyer lemon segments, supremed

4 teaspoons micro fennel fronds

Freshly ground pepper

# Asparagus, Carrot, Corn, and Celery Root Soups

*These four delightful soups, each one an outstanding showcase for its featured ingredient, are relatively simple to prepare and can be served individually or as a quartet. They display elegance and refinement, yet all possess a homey deliciousness.*

**Method**—*To make the Celery Root Soup:* In a high-speed blender, combine the water, celery root, celery, olive oil, and lemon juice and purée until smooth. Pass through a fine-mesh sieve and season to taste with salt and pepper.

*To make the garnish for the Celery Root Soup:* Combine the celery root slices, coriander, and olive oil in a bowl and toss to mix. Season to taste with salt and pepper. Cover and refrigerate overnight, then julienne the slices just before serving.

Sprinkle the eggplant slices with salt, place on a plate, and refrigerate for 1 day. The next day, rinse the slices and squeeze out the liquid. Place in a shallow bowl, cover with the vinegar, and refrigerate for 1 more day. The next day, drain, squeeze the slices to extract the excess liquid, return to the bowl, and add the basil, garlic, and olive oil. Refrigerate for at least 2 hours before using. (The eggplant can be held in the refrigerator for up to 1 week.) Cut the eggplant into small wedges and discard the basil and garlic.

*To make the Corn Soup:* In the high-speed blender, combine the corn and water and purée until smooth. Pass through a fine-mesh sieve and season to taste with salt and pepper.

*To make the garnish for the Corn Soup:* Spread the corn kernels on a dehydrator shelf and dehydrate at 105°F for 2 hours, or until dry but tender. Ready the heart of palm and Curry Oil and reserve until serving.

*To make the Asparagus Soup:* In the high-speed blender, combine the water, asparagus, avocado, celery, olive oil, shoyu, lemon juice, onion, garlic, thyme, tarragon, and cayenne and purée until smooth. Pass through a fine-mesh sieve and season to taste with salt and black pepper.

*To make the garnish for the Asparagus Soup:* Ready the asparagus tips, white asparagus, fennel, and Herb Oil and reserve until serving.

*To make the Carrot Soup:* In a heavy-duty juicer, juice the carrots. Discard the pulp, measure out 2 cups juice, and immediately pour the juice into the high-speed blender. Add the avocado, coconut meat, garlic, and lemon juice and purée until smooth. Season to taste with salt and pepper.

*To make the garnish for the Carrot Soup:* Ready the olive oil and sesame seeds and reserve until serving.

**Assembly**—Divide each soup among 4 bowls. Garnish each soup with its garnishes.

**Wine Notes**—Four different soups and only one wine—it sounds like a job for Riesling! This course calls for the versatility present in a racy German Kabinett. The touch of spicy sweetness and the richness in the corn soup are handled with grace by the Riesling, as is the higher acidity of the celery root soup. Look for such incredible producers as Fritz Haag and von Hovel from the Mosel and Donnhoff from Nahe.

**Serves 4**

## Celery Root Soup

2 cups filtered water

2 cups chopped celery root

$^1/_4$ cup chopped celery

2 tablespoons extra virgin olive oil

1 teaspoon freshly squeezed
lemon juice

Celtic sea salt and freshly
ground pepper

## Garnish for Celery Root Soup

2 thin slices celery root

$^1/_4$ teaspoon freshly
ground coriander

2 tablespoons olive oil

Celtic sea salt and freshly
ground pepper

2 $^1/_4$-inch-thick slices eggplant

$^1/_2$ cup rice wine vinegar

6 fresh basil leaves, chopped

3 cloves garlic, smashed

$^1/_3$ cup extra virgin olive oil

## Corn Soup

3 cups sweet corn kernels

1 cup filtered water

Celtic sea salt and freshly
ground pepper

## Garnish for Corn Soup

$^1/_2$ cup sweet corn kernels

$^1/_4$ cup julienned heart of palm

4 teaspoons Curry Oil
(see Appendices)

## Asparagus Soup

1 $^1/_2$ cups filtered water

2 cups chopped asparagus

$^1/_2$ avocado, peeled and chopped

$^1/_4$ cup chopped celery

2 tablespoons extra virgin olive oil

2 tablespoons nama shoyu

2 teaspoons freshly squeezed
lemon juice

2 teaspoons minced onion

1 teaspoon minced garlic

Leaves from 1 thyme sprig

1 $^1/_2$ teaspoons fresh
tarragon leaves

Pinch of freshly ground
cayenne pepper

Celtic sea salt and freshly
ground black pepper

## Garnish for Asparagus Soup

8 asparagus tips, each sliced
lengthwise into thirds

1 stalk white asparagus, thinly
sliced on the diagonal

4 tablespoons shaved fennel

4 teaspoons Herb Oil
(see Appendices)

## Carrot Soup

8 juicing carrots, peeled

$^1/_2$ avocado, peeled and chopped

2 tablespoons chopped young
Thai coconut meat

1 teaspoon minced garlic

Juice of $^1/_2$ lemon

Celtic sea salt and freshly
ground pepper

## Garnish for Carrot Soup

4 teaspoons extra virgin olive oil

2 teaspoons white sesame seeds

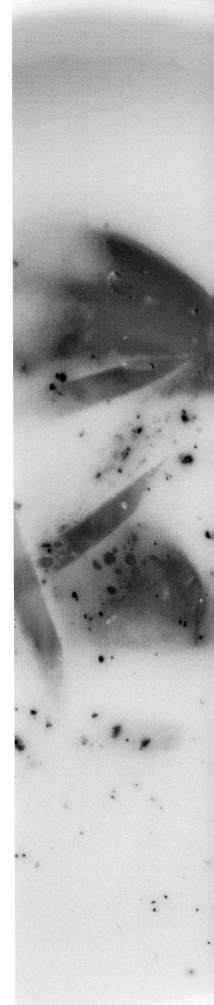

CARROT SOUP

CELERY ROOT SOUP

CORN SOUP

ASPARAGUS SOUP

# SALADS

# Greek Salad

*Creamy, slightly sour feta "cheese," the star of the dish, laces together all the other elements. The Pickled Garlic also plays an important role, supplying a complex flavor that gives the salad depth.*

**Method**—*To make the Almond Feta Cheese:* Using a high-speed blender or a Champion juicer with the blank screen in place, combine the almonds and Rejuvelac and process until a very thick paste forms. Add a splash of filtered water if too thick. Pour the mixture onto a double thickness of cheesecloth, bring the corners together, and squeeze out the remaining "whey." Transfer the paste to a sieve placed over a bowl. Cover the sieve with a kitchen towel, and set the bowl aside in a warm place for 12 to 14 hours. The mixture will develop the texture of a soft fresh goat cheese.

Add the nutritional yeast, lemon juice, onion, and salt to the almond mixture and mix with a plastic spatula. Using an offset spatula, form the mixture into a small block $^3/_4$ inch thick. Place the block on a nonstick drying sheet on a dehydrator shelf and dehydrate at 105°F for 6 hours. Flip the block off the drying sheet onto the dehydrator shelf and dehydrate for 2 hours longer. Cut the block into $^1/_2$-inch cubes, and separate the cubes. Continue to dehydrate for 4 hours longer. The cubes should have the consistency of baked tofu.

*To make the vinaigrette:* Whisk together the vinegar and olive oil in a bowl. Just before using, stir in the thyme, oregano, and shallot and season to taste with salt and pepper.

Toss all the beans with all but 2 tablespoons of the vinaigrette and season to taste with salt and pepper. Toss the lettuce with half of the olives, the cinnamon, clove, crushed garlic, and reserved vinaigrette.

*To make the Tomato Juice Garnish:* Pass the tomatoes through a fine-mesh sieve placed over a small bowl. Whisk in the olive oil, season to taste with salt and pepper, and fold in the parsley.

**Assembly**—Combine the beans, cherry tomato slices, cucumber slices, and the remaining olives in a bowl and toss to mix. Using a slotted spoon, place some of the bean mixture in the center of each plate. Arrange one-fourth of the lettuce leaves over the beans. Spoon the tomato garnish around the plate and sprinkle with the Pickled Garlic slices and cheese cubes. Top with pepper. Drizzle any vinaigrette remaining in the bowl that held the beans around the plate.

**Wine Notes**—All you need to complete this dish are a crisp Sauvignon Blanc and a warm summer evening. Brander's Au Naturel from California's Santa Barbara has the bracing acidity and herbal notes to complement the vinaigrette and greens. Greek wine is also an obvious choice with this course. The citrus notes of a lively Assyrtiko would brighten the flavors of the vinaigrette.

## Serves 4

### Almond Feta Cheese

2 cups raw almonds, soaked for 2 hours in filtered water, drained, and peeled

$^3/_4$ cup Rejuvelac (see Appendices)

4 teaspoons large flake nutritional yeast

1 teaspoon freshly squeezed lemon juice

1 tablespoon minced onion

$^1/_2$ teaspoon Celtic sea salt

### Vinaigrette

2 tablespoons red wine vinegar

$^1/_4$ cup extra virgin olive oil

1 $^1/_2$ teaspoons finely chopped fresh thyme

1 $^1/_2$ teaspoons finely chopped fresh oregano

1 teaspoon finely diced shallot

Celtic sea salt and freshly ground pepper

2 ounces haricots verts

2 ounces thin yellow wax beans

2 ounces thin purple beans

Celtic sea salt and freshly ground pepper

24 small romaine lettuce leaves from the heart of the head

$^1/_2$ pound Kalamata olives, pitted and chopped

1 teaspoon freshly ground cinnamon

1 teaspoon freshly ground clove

2 Pickled Garlic cloves (see Appendices), crushed

### Tomato Juice Garnish

$^1/_4$ cup very finely chopped mixed red and yellow tomatoes

1 tablespoon extra virgin olive oil

Celtic sea salt and freshly ground pepper

1 teaspoon chopped fresh flat-leaf parsley

3 ounces red cherry tomatoes, sliced crosswise $^1/_8$ inch thick

3 ounces yellow cherry tomatoes, sliced crosswise $^1/_8$ inch thick

16 thin slices English cucumber ($^1/_8$ inch thick)

2 Pickled Garlic cloves (see Appendices), very thinly sliced

Freshly ground pepper

# Marinated Artichokes, Turnips, and Beets with Date and Cranberry Purées

*The idea behind this preparation is to combine the sharp and assertive flavors of artichokes and turnips with the sweet and comforting flavors of dates and cranberries. With the first taste, all seems straightforward, but as you begin to chew and swallow, a surprising depth — almost like a great wine — lingers on the palate. The coup de grace comes in the form of the jalapeño-laced vinaigrette, as it cuts through and ultimately weaves together all the components, while mâche and sea salt further dance about the tongue.*

**Method**—*To make the Date Purée:* In a high-speed blender, combine the dates, water, and orange juice and process until smooth. Pass the purée through a fine-mesh sieve and season to taste with salt and pepper.

*To make the Cranberry Purée:* In the high-speed blender, combine the cranberries, water, and lemon juice and process until smooth. Pass the purée through a fine-mesh sieve and season to taste with salt and pepper.

*To make the Jalapeño Vinaigrette:* Combine the chile, olive oil, vinegar, and chives in a mortar and gently grind with a pestle. Season to taste with salt and pepper.

Place the red and golden beets, the turnip, and the artichoke slices in separate bowls. Whisk together the olive oil, vinegar, and salt and pepper to taste in a small bowl and divide evenly among the vegetables. Toss to coat.

**Assembly**—Place a circle of the Cranberry Purée at 12 o'clock and a circle of the Date Purée at 6 o'clock on each plate. Roll the beet slices into cones and arrange over the purées. Place some artichoke and turnip slices in among the beets. Sprinkle the mâche leaves over the vegetables. Spoon the vinaigrette around the 2 circles of purée.

**Wine Notes**—When the elements of this dish are eaten separately, it seems as if you might need three or four different wines to accompany them. There is sweetness in the dates, the Cranberry Purée sings with acidity, and the unusual flavor of artichokes is almost always a wine-pairing problem. If all of the ingredients are tasted together, however, the dish walks the tightrope of perfect balance. An Alsatian Pinot Gris from Josmeyer, which is not an overripe or excessively sweet style, enhances the many flavors and textures of the dish.

**Serves 4**

**Date Purée**

$1/2$ cup firmly packed, pitted Medjool dates

$1/2$ cup filtered water

2 tablespoons freshly squeezed orange juice

Celtic sea salt and freshly ground pepper

**Cranberry Purée**

$1/2$ cup dried cranberries

$1/4$ cup filtered water

1 tablespoon freshly squeezed lemon juice

Celtic sea salt and freshly ground pepper

**Jalapeño Vinaigrette**

1 jalapeño chile, seeded and chopped

$1/4$ cup extra virgin olive oil

1 tablespoon white wine vinegar

1 tablespoon chopped fresh chives

Celtic sea salt and freshly ground pepper

1 small red beet, peeled and thinly sliced

1 small golden (yellow) beet, peeled and thinly sliced

1 small red turnip, peeled and thinly sliced

1 artichoke bottom, choke and stem removed, bottom thinly sliced vertically, and slices coated with freshly squeezed lemon juice

$1/4$ cup extra virgin olive oil

4 teaspoons sherry wine vinegar

Celtic sea salt and freshly ground pepper

1 cup mâche leaves

# Morel Mushrooms and Lotus Root with Beets and Fermented Black Beans

*The meaty texture of the morels contrasts marvelously with the barely crunchy lotus root. The emulsion of puréed beets adds an ethereal note of sweetness, while the fermented black beans furnish an important pungency. Small shiso leaves help to balance this humble, yet at the same time exciting, blend of ingredients.*

**Method**—*To prepare the mushrooms:* Combine the mushrooms, water, and vinegar in a bowl and let soak for 1 hour to rehydrate. Remove the mushrooms from the liquid, reserving the liquid. Cut the mushrooms in half lengthwise. Using a high-speed blender, combine 8 mushroom halves and about $1/2$ cup of the reserved liquid and process until very smooth, adding more of the liquid as needed. Season to taste with salt and pepper. Season the remaining mushroom halves to taste with salt and pepper.

*To prepare the lotus root:* Combine the lotus root, olive oil, citron juice, and lime juice in a bowl and toss to mix. Cover and refrigerate for 2 hours. Remove the lotus root slices from the liquid just before using. Season the slices to taste with salt and pepper.

*To make the Beet Emulsion:* Using a heavy-duty juicer, juice the beets. Discard the pulp and allow the juice to settle for about 1 hour; a thick layer of froth will form on the top.

*To make the Fermented Black Bean Vinaigrette:* Rinse the beans in 20 changes of clean, cold water, then squeeze out the excess liquid. Chop the beans and place in a bowl. Add the currants, vinegar, and olive oil and stir to combine. Season to taste with salt and pepper.

**Assembly**—Using one-fourth of the mushroom purée, first spoon some of it in an elongated oval in the center of each plate, and then spoon a diagonal line of purée through the oval. Layer one-fourth of the morel mushroom halves and lotus root slices in the center of the oval. Using one-fourth of the Beet Emulsion, spoon some of it on top of the stacked mushrooms and lotus root and then at 4 points around the plate. Drizzle one-fourth of the vinaigrette around the plate and sprinkle with 1 teaspoon of the shiso.

**Wine Notes**—Rosé wines are often underappreciated and are usually associated with the innocuous white Zinfandels of the world. World-class rosés not only excite the palate, but can also pair with certain dishes whites and reds cannot. The Tablas Creek Rosé from Paso Robles is made in the style of a wine from the southern Rhône, utilizing Mourvèdre, Grenache, and Counoise grapes. The morel mushrooms have been marinated in balsamic vinegar, which calls for a wine with a good level of acid, a characteristic of the Tablas Creek. Also, the Beet Emulsion especially highlights the strawberry and raspberry elements of this distinctive rosé.

**Serves 4**

**Mushrooms**

16 large dried morel mushrooms

$1/2$ cup filtered water

$1/2$ cup Villa Manodori balsamic vinegar

Celtic sea salt and freshly ground pepper

**Lotus Root**

16 thin slices lotus root

2 tablespoons extra virgin olive oil

1 tablespoon yuzu citron juice

2 teaspoons freshly squeezed lime juice

Celtic sea salt and freshly ground pepper

**Beet Emulsion**

2 large red beets, peeled and chopped

**Fermented Black Bean Vinaigrette**

$1/4$ cup fermented black beans

1 tablespoon dried black currants, chopped

2 teaspoons sherry wine vinegar

2 tablespoons extra virgin arbequina olive oil

Celtic sea salt and freshly ground pepper

4 teaspoons micro shiso leaves

# Carpaccio of Artichokes, Bleeding Heart Radish, Carrots, and Golden Beets

*This distinctive and remarkably simple carpaccio celebrates the pure flavor of each vegetable. All of them are served without fuss, treated to only a minimum of aromatics and seasonings. One possibility is to offer just one or two of the vegetables; the other is to offer them all. Sometimes the best way to experience a vegetable is to compare it side by side with others.*

**Method**—*To prepare the artichoke:* Combine the artichoke, olive oil, and lemon juice in a bowl and toss to mix. Season to taste with salt and pepper.

*To prepare the radish:* Combine the radish slices, citron juice, and sesame oil in a bowl and toss to mix. Season to taste with salt and pepper. Lay the slices flat. Mix together the wasabi and apple in a small bowl. Spread some of the mixture over each radish slice.

*To prepare the carrot:* Combine the carrot, olive oil, and vinegar in a bowl and toss to mix. Season to taste with salt and pepper.

*To prepare the beet:* Combine the beet, ginger, garlic, shallot, olive oil, and vinegar in a bowl and toss to mix. Season to taste with salt and pepper

**Assembly**—For each serving, arrange one-fourth of each vegetable on a small plate, overlapping the pieces and, in the case of the golden beet, rolling the slices into cones. Spoon any of the remaining juices from each vegetable on the respective vegetable. Sprinkle the parsley evenly over the artichoke, the mint evenly over the radish, the dill evenly over the carrot, and the chives evenly over the beet. Sprinkle all the vegetables with pepper.

**Wine Notes**—A vast array of flavors is present in this dish, and although it might seem a daunting prospect to choose a single wine to accompany all four elements, a reasonable and realistic choice is possible. Champagne anyone? A crisp Blanc de Blancs from Pierre Peters or Larmandier-Bernier is not only incredible juice in its own right, but also highlights the individual zip that each of these vegetables displays.

Serves 4

### Artichoke

1 artichoke bottom, choke and stem removed and bottom thinly sliced vertically

1 tablespoon extra virgin olive oil

1 tablespoon freshly squeezed lemon juice

Celtic sea salt and freshly ground pepper

### Bleeding Heart Radish

1 small bleeding heart radish, peeled and thinly sliced into rounds

1 tablespoon yuzu citron juice

1 tablespoon cold-pressed sesame oil

Celtic sea salt and freshly ground pepper

$1/4$ teaspoon freshly grated wasabi

2 teaspoons grated, peeled apple

### Carrot

1 carrot, thinly sliced on the diagonal

2 tablespoons extra virgin olive oil

2 teaspoons red wine vinegar

Celtic sea salt and freshly ground pepper

### Golden Beet

1 small golden (yellow) beet, peeled and thinly sliced

$1/2$ teaspoon finely minced, peeled fresh ginger

$1/2$ teaspoon finely minced garlic

$1/2$ teaspoon finely minced shallot

2 tablespoons extra virgin olive oil

2 teaspoons rice wine vinegar

Celtic sea salt and freshly ground pepper

### Garnish

2 teaspoons fresh flat-leaf parsley leaves, cut into fine chiffonade

4 teaspoons fresh micro mint leaves

1 teaspoon chopped fresh dill

1 tablespoon $1/2$-inch-long-cut fresh chives

Freshly ground pepper

# Corn, Jicama, Asian Pear, and Cucumber Salad with Avocado Purée

*This combination of corn, jicama, Asian pear, and cucumber tossed together with a lively Lime Vinaigrette sparkles with flavor. With the addition of chopped jalapeño, mint, and flat-leaf parsley, the medley of tastes becomes even more interesting. A final touch of Avocado Purée delivers a sensuous creaminess that rounds out the dish perfectly.*

**Method**—*To make the salad:* Combine the jicama, corn, cucumber, pear, olive oil, lime juice, chile, mint, and parsley in a bowl and toss to mix. Season to taste with salt and pepper.

*To make the Avocado Purée:* In a high-speed blender, combine the avocado, lime juice, and water and purée until smooth. Season to taste with salt and pepper.

*To make the Lime Vinaigrette:* Whisk together the lime juice and olive oil in a bowl. Season to taste with salt and pepper and stir in the lime pieces.

**Assembly**—Spoon a vertical line of the Avocado Purée on the center of each plate. Spoon on 2 additional lines, making them perpendicular to the first line and crossing it. Position 1 of the lines one-third from the top of the first line, and position the other line two-thirds from the top of the first line. Spoon some of the salad to the left of the intersecting points of the lines, placing it on the purée. Drizzle the vinaigrette over the salad and around the plate, and sprinkle with the parsley, mint, and lime zest.

**Wine Notes**—When most people think of German Riesling, the first thing that comes to mind are sweet wines from the Piesporter and Blue Nun era. Yet a majority of the wines from the top German producers are actually trocken, or dry styles. Robert Weil's trocken Rieslings from the Rheingau are the perfect accent for the brightness and freshness of this dish. The lime-laced vinaigrette makes the salad sing with acidity, and the coolness and minerality of the cucumbers complement the flavors of the Riesling.

## Serves 4

### Salad

1/4 cup brunoise-cut jicama

1/4 cup sweet corn kernels

1/4 cup brunoise-cut, skin-on English cucumber

1/4 cup brunoise-cut, peeled Asian pear

1 tablespoon extra virgin olive oil

4 teaspoons freshly squeezed lime juice

1 tablespoon minced jalapeño chile

1 tablespoon chopped fresh mint

2 teaspoons finely chopped fresh flat-leaf parsley

Celtic sea salt and freshly ground pepper

### Avocado Purée

1/2 avocado, peeled and chopped

2 teaspoons freshly squeezed lime juice

1/4 cup filtered water

Celtic sea salt and freshly ground pepper

### Lime Vinaigrette

1 1/2 tablespoons freshly squeezed lime juice

1/4 cup extra virgin olive oil

Celtic sea salt and freshly ground pepper

4 lime segments, supremed and cut into thirds

2 teaspoons chopped fresh flat-leaf parsley

2 teaspoons fresh micro mint leaves

2 teaspoons finely grated lime zest

# Watermelon Salad

*A tremendous complexity of texture and flavor is present in this salad, even though it initially seems rather straightforward. The clean, assertive bite of the horseradish perfectly cuts through the micro greens, watermelon, and longans, while at the same time not overpowering any of them. Olive oil and black pepper round out the dish with a smooth richness and a poignant heat, respectively. Also, because this preparation is light, it is an excellent way to start out a multicourse feast.*

**Method**—Using a high-speed blender, process the chopped watermelon until it is a medium-bodied liquid. Allow the juice to settle, about 10 minutes; a thick layer of froth will form on the top.

Place the watermelon squares on a work surface, and top each square with a single layer of longan pieces, covering each square completely.

**Assembly**—Place a watermelon square in the center of each plate and arrange one-fourth of the micro greens over the longans. Sprinkle 1 teaspoon of the grated horseradish over the micro greens. Drizzle the olive oil around the plate and spoon some of the watermelon froth around the plate and over the greens. Sprinkle the remaining grated horseradish over the watermelon froth. Top with a little salt and pepper.

**Wine Notes**—At first thought it would seem that the spicy horseradish would require a lot of attention, but in fact it is a delicate background flavor that melts into the rest of the dish. This wonderfully refreshing preparation must have a wine partner that has the same cleansing characteristics. Laurent-Perrier's Brut Rosé Champagne has scents of fresh berries and yeastiness and an invigorating sparkle that enlivens the watermelon and longans on the palate.

**Serves 4**

2 cups chopped red watermelon

4 pieces red watermelon, each 3 inches square and $1/2$ inch thick

12 longans, peeled, pitted, and cut into eighths

1 cup assorted micro greens such as shiso, basil, and chervil

4 teaspoons freshly grated horseradish

2 tablespoons extra virgin olive oil

Celtic sea salt and freshly ground pepper

# Savory Fruit Salad

*The flavors in the salad preparation are simple and satisfying. Melon and nectarine provide a sensual richness that is superbly tamed by the sharp notes of the red onion and mustard. A vinaigrette featuring fennel, olive oil, and lemon juice is all that is required to complete this superb harmony of ingredients. Other melons, peaches, figs, or apricots could be used in addition to or in lieu of the suggested fruits.*

**Method**—*To make the Fennel Vinaigrette:* Combine the brunoise-cut fennel, the fennel fronds, olive oil, lemon juice, and shallot in a bowl and stir to mix. Season to taste with salt and pepper.

*To make the salad:* Combine the onion, lime juice, and a little salt and pepper in a bowl and marinate for 30 minutes. Just before serving, combine the marinated onion, the melon, nectarine, shaved fennel, and mustard seeds in a bowl and toss gently to mix. Season to taste with salt and pepper.

**Assembly**—Arrange one-fourth of the salad in the center of each plate, topping off the salad with some of the red onion pieces. Spoon the Fennel Vinaigrette around the plate, and sprinkle each salad with 1 teaspoon of the chervil.

**Wine Notes**—For the sweetness of the melon and nectarines, as well as the acidity from the Fennel Vinaigrette, only a wine with residual sugar will do. A Vouvray demi-sec will enliven the Sharlyn melon and also balance with the brightness of the vinaigrette. Producers with a more opulent style, such as Philippe Foreau or Gaston Huet, are particularly interesting.

**Serves 4**

**Fennel Vinaigrette**

$1/3$ cup brunoise-cut fennel

1 teaspoon chopped fennel fronds

2 tablespoons extra virgin olive oil

2 teaspoons freshly squeezed lemon juice

1 teaspoon minced shallot

Celtic sea salt and freshly ground pepper

**Salad**

$1/4$ cup finely julienned red onion

1 tablespoon freshly squeezed lime juice

Celtic sea salt and freshly ground pepper

1 cup very thinly sliced Sharlyn melon

1 nectarine, peeled, pitted, and thinly sliced

$1/2$ cup shaved fennel

$1/2$ teaspoon mustard seeds

4 teaspoons micro chervil sprigs

# Tomato, Rapini, and Spring Legume Salad

*This seasonal salad features a combination of strikingly pleasant crunchy vegetables. The rapini, legumes, and fennel are superbly subdued by the sharp Mustard Vinaigrette. Pieces of tomato add a sweet acidity that further tames the vegetables and also provide a soft, meaty texture to contrast with the crunchiness.*

**Method**—*To prepare the rapini:* Place the rapini in a bowl and drizzle the vinegar over it. Marinate for 30 minutes. Season to taste with salt and pepper.

*To prepare the legumes:* Combine the purple beans, wax beans, haricots verts, tomato, fennel, garlic, parsley, and olive oil and toss to mix. Season to taste with salt and pepper.

*To make the Mustard Vinaigrette:* Combine the mustard seeds and 2 tablespoons of the vinegar in a bowl and let soak for 1 hour. Drain the mustard seeds and put them in a mortar. Add the olive oil and the remaining 1 tablespoon vinegar and gently crush the mustard seeds with a pestle until all the elements are fully incorporated.

**Assembly**—Combine the rapini, legumes, and arugula in a bowl and toss to mix. Season to taste with salt and pepper. Place a mound of the legume salad in the center of each plate. Spoon the Mustard Vinaigrette around the plate and sprinkle with the daikon sprouts.

**Wine Notes**—The green flavors of arugula and rapini lead this course to a crisp Sauvignon Blanc. The Marlborough region of New Zealand, one of the wine world's most exciting areas today, is home to aromatic, zingy Sauvignon Blanc with distinctive grassy, gooseberry notes. Marlborough's Seresin produces one of the region's top Sauvignon Blancs, and it performed like a megaphone with the haricots verts and arugula.

**Serves 4**

### Rapini

12 small pieces rapini

1 tablespoon red wine vinegar

Celtic sea salt and freshly ground pepper

### Legumes

12 purple beans, cut crosswise into thirds

12 yellow wax beans, cut crosswise into thirds

12 haricots verts

1 red heirloom tomato, peeled, seeded, and cut into small wedges

1/2 cup julienned fennel

2 cloves elephant garlic, sliced paper-thin, soaked for 1 hour in filtered water, and drained

1 1/2 tablespoons chopped fresh flat-leaf parsley

2 tablespoons extra virgin olive oil

Celtic sea salt and freshly ground pepper

### Mustard Vinaigrette

2 tablespoons mustard seeds, soaked for 10 to 12 hours in filtered water and drained

3 tablespoons white wine vinegar

3 tablespoons extra virgin olive oil

1 cup baby arugula

Celtic sea salt and freshly ground pepper

2 tablespoons plus 2 teaspoons micro daikon sprouts

# Arugula Caesar Salad

*By substituting arugula for the usual romaine in this Caesar, we end up with a more grown-up combination of flavors. The croutons and Rawmesan offer comforting notes, while the arugula provides spicy, cleansing elements—qualities that are repeated with a drizzle of chile oil at the finish. A creamy yet pungent dressing pulls everything together with memorable flair.*

**Method**—*To make the Gnocchi Croutons:* Peel the carrot and, using a vegetable peeler, cut it lengthwise into thin strips. Arrange the strips on a dehydrator shelf and dehydrate at 105°F for 8 hours, or until completely dry. Break the dried strips into small pieces, place in a spice grinder, and grind to a fine powder.

Meanwhile, combine the Cashew Cheese, nutritional yeast, lemon juice, red onion, miso, yellow onion, salt, white pepper, and nutmeg in a bowl and stir until all the ingredients are evenly incorporated. Chill the mixture for 1 hour to make it easier to handle.

When the crouton mixture is ready, roll it into ropes $^1/_2$ inch in diameter. Cut the ropes into $^1/_2$-inch-long pieces. Gently toss the croutons in the carrot powder, coating evenly on all sides. Place the croutons on a nonstick drying sheet on a dehydrator shelf and dehydrate at 105°F for 4 hours, or until crisp on the outside and soft on the inside.

*To make the Caesar Dressing:* In a high-speed blender, combine all the ingredients and process until the mixture is the consistency of a conventional Caesar dressing. Taste and adjust the seasoning. Measure out $^3/_4$ to 1 cup of the dressing to use for the salad. Reserve the remainder for another use; it will keep tightly capped in the refrigerator for up to 2 weeks.

**Assembly**—Place the arugula in a bowl, drizzle on the olive oil, and toss to coat the leaves evenly. Season to taste with salt and pepper and toss again. Arrange the arugula leaves, overlapping them, in the center of each plate. Sprinkle the croutons and Rawmesan around the arugula. Spoon 3 to 4 tablespoons of the dressing around the plate, and then drizzle 1 teaspoon of the chile oil around the plate. Season lightly with salt and pepper.

**Wine Notes**—This is a rich, full-flavored dish because of the croutons and the Caesar Dressing. A wine-pairing complexity arises from the high acidity of the dressing and the green, nutty flavors of the arugula. A successful wine needs to have a touch of oak aging, but remain crisp and racy. Chablis made by Domaine Laroche, which boasts particularly exciting wines from its Vaillons and Les Vaudevey Vineyards, has the right combination.

**Serves 4**

**Gnocchi Croutons**

1 carrot

1 cup Cashew Cheese
(see Appendices)

1 $^1/_2$ teaspoons large flake
nutritional yeast

1 tablespoon freshly squeezed
lemon juice

1 tablespoon minced red onion

1 tablespoon white miso

1 teaspoon minced yellow onion

1 teaspoon Celtic sea salt

Pinch of freshly ground
white pepper

Pinch of freshly grated nutmeg

**Caesar Dressing**

1 cup extra virgin olive oil

3 cloves garlic

2 medium celery stalks, chopped

$^1/_2$ cup filtered water

$^1/_4$ cup freshly squeezed lemon juice

$^1/_4$ cup nama shoyu

2 tablespoons white miso

4 teaspoons Date Paste
(see Appendices)

1 tablespoon kelp granules

$^1/_2$ teaspoon freshly ground pepper

$^3/_4$ pound baby arugula

1 tablespoon extra virgin olive oil

Celtic sea salt and freshly
ground pepper

$^1/_2$ cup Rawmesan (see Appendices)

4 teaspoons chile oil

# Heirloom Tomato Terrine and Salad

*These two tomato preparations, both of which celebrate the glorious flavors of the tomato, can be served individually or combined. Whereas the terrine emphasizes the lusciousness and meatiness of the heirloom tomatoes, the salad showcases the concentrated sweetness of the dehydrated tomato pieces. Mâche in whole and puréed forms and balsamic vinegar are the common denominators of the two dishes.*

**Method**—*To make the terrine:* Peel and quarter the red and yellow tomatoes through the stem end, then cut away the core and seed pockets. Cut perfect rectangles 1 $^1/_2$ inches long and as wide as the tomato quarters allow. Line a 6 by 1 $^1/_2$ by 2 $^1/_4$-inch metal terrine mold with detachable sides with plastic wrap, allowing an overhang on the long sides. Place a layer of the red tomato pieces in the terrine mold, and press down to create a flat layer. Season with salt and pepper. Place a layer of the yellow tomatoes over the red tomatoes and season with salt and pepper. Continue the layering process until you have reached the top of the mold. Cover with the overhanging plastic wrap and press down firmly. Refrigerate for 1 hour. Detach the mold sides, remove the plastic-wrapped terrine from the mold, and tighten the plastic wrap by pulling a long edge taut. With the plastic wrap still in place, cut the terrine into 12 slices each about $^1/_2$ inch thick. Carefully remove the plastic wrap from each slice. The layers may shift slightly, but you can easily push them back together. Select the 8 nicest slices for serving (the end slices are usually raggedy, and some of the others may not want to hold together, thus the need to cut 12 slices).

*To make the Tomato Chips:* Place the tomato slices on a nonstick drying sheet on a dehydrator shelf and, using a brush, coat lightly with the olive oil. Dehydrate at 105°F for 6 to 8 hours, or until dry. Remove the slices from the drying sheet while they are still warm, using a spatula if necessary to loosen them. Let cool completely, then store in an airtight container at room temperature until ready to use.

*To make the Mâche Purée:* In a mortar, combine the mâche and olive oil. Grind with a pestle to create a coarse purée. Season to taste with salt and pepper.

*To make the Tomato and Mâche Salad:* Place the tomato pieces on a nonstick drying sheet on a dehydrator shelf and dehydrate at 105°F for 3 hours, or until the exterior is dry and the interior is tender. Combine the tomato pieces, mâche, and olive oil in a bowl and toss to mix. Season to taste with salt and pepper.

**Assembly**—For each serving, have 2 small plates. Spoon one-eighth of the Mâche Purée in a pool in the center of the first plate, and place a slice of the tomato terrine over the purée. Sprinkle a little salt on the terrine and drizzle $^1/_2$ teaspoon of the vinegar around the purée. On the second plate, place one-eighth of the Tomato and Mâche Salad. Stand a few Tomato Chips upright on the salad. Spoon $^1/_2$ teaspoon of the vinegar, $^3/_4$ teaspoon of the olive oil, and 1 teaspoon of the Basil Oil around the salad. Sprinkle the salad with salt and pepper.

**Wine Notes**—Eroica, a collaboration between Dr. Ernst Loosen of Germany and Chateau Ste. Michelle of Washington State, is a Columbia Valley Riesling that skillfully handles the twists and turns of this dish. The tomato terrine and the aged balsamic vinegar both have sweetness that is exquisitely balanced by the Riesling.

**Serves 8**

**Terrine**

5 or 6 large,
red heirloom tomatoes

5 or 6 large,
yellow heirloom tomatoes

Celtic sea salt and freshly
ground pepper

**Tomato Chips**

2 golf ball–sized red tomatoes,
cut into $\frac{1}{8}$-inch-thick slices

2 golf ball–sized yellow tomatoes,
cut into $\frac{1}{8}$-inch-thick slices

1 tablespoon extra virgin olive oil

**Mâche Purée**

1 cup chopped mâche

1 tablespoon extra virgin olive oil

Celtic sea salt and freshly
ground pepper

**Tomato and Mâche Salad**

2 small, yellow heirloom tomatoes,
peeled, halved, seeded, and cut
into eighths

2 small, red heirloom tomatoes,
peeled, halved, seeded, and cut
into eighths

2 cups mâche leaves

2 tablespoons extra virgin olive oil

Celtic sea salt and freshly
ground pepper

Celtic sea salt

8 teaspoons 25-year-old
Villa Manodori balsamic vinegar

2 tablespoons extra virgin olive oil

8 teaspoons Basil Oil
(see Appendices)

Freshly ground pepper

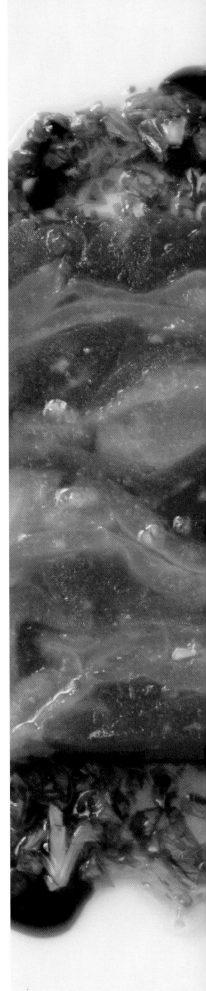

HEIRLOOM TOMATO TERRINE AND SALAD

# Mediterranean Cheese Salad with Dragon Crackers

*The cashew-based cheese in this dish is distinguished by itself, but it goes to another level when crusted with sun-dried tomatoes and black olives, two assertive ingredients that highlight its complexity. A fresh-tomato vinaigrette, Garlic Chips, and Spicy Pine Nuts add additional depth of flavor and texture. Lastly, Dragon Crackers made from flaxseed are loaded with flavor and deliver the perfect crunchy backdrop, definitively weaving everything together.*

**Method**—*To make the Cheese Log:* Shape the cheese into a log about 6 inches long and 2 inches in diameter. In a shallow pan, combine the sun-dried tomatoes, olives, and basil. Roll the log in the mixture and place in a shallow rectangular pan. Pour in the olive oil, cover, and refrigerate for 8 hours to firm up before slicing.

*To make the Spicy Pine Nuts:* Combine all the ingredients in a bowl and toss to mix. Spread on a dehydrator shelf and dehydrate at 105°F for 24 hours, or until crisp. Set aside 4 tablespoons to use for the salad; reserve the remainder for another use.

*To make the Tomato Vinaigrette:* Combine the tomatoes, olives, olive oil, and vinegar in a bowl and toss to mix. Season to taste with salt and pepper.

**Assembly**—Remove the Cheese Log from the oil and cut it crosswise into 4 equal slices. Place 1 slice in the center of each plate. Spoon one-fourth of the vinaigrette evenly around the plate. Sprinkle with 1 tablespoon pine nuts, 1 teaspoon Basil Oil, 1/2 teaspoon Garlic Chips, and 1 tablespoon micro basil. Place 2 Dragon Crackers alongside the cheese. Top with pepper.

**Wine Notes**—The Cashew Cheese is packed with flavor and power. If the cheese was served by itself, this course would require a fuller-bodied wine with strong tannins and explosive fruit. By rolling it in olives and adding the Tomato Vinaigrette, the course actually becomes lighter and livelier. Wine-wise we can move to a more elegant and feminine choice with higher acidity. The cool climate of California's Anderson Valley produces this style of Pinot Noir, with Littorai's Savoy Vineyard and Handley bottling some of the best.

**Serves 4**

### Cheese Log

2 cups Cashew Cheese (see Appendices)

1/2 cup chopped, drained olive oil–packed sun-dried tomatoes

1/2 cup chopped, pitted Kalamata olives

2 tablespoons chopped fresh basil

2 cups extra virgin olive oil

### Spicy Pine Nuts

1 cup raw pine nuts, soaked for 8 to 10 hours in filtered water and drained

2 teaspoons chili powder

1 1/2 teaspoons minced onion

3/4 teaspoon freshly ground cumin

1/4 teaspoon freshly ground cayenne pepper

1/2 teaspoon Celtic sea salt

### Tomato Vinaigrette

2 green zebra tomatoes, cut into eighths

6 red grape tomatoes, quartered

6 yellow grape tomatoes, quartered

2 tablespoons chopped, pitted Kalamata olives

2 tablespoons extra virgin olive oil

2 teaspoons red wine vinegar

Celtic sea salt and freshly ground pepper

4 teaspoons Basil Oil (see Appendices)

2 teaspoons Garlic Chips (see Appendices), broken

4 tablespoons fresh micro purple and green basil leaves

8 Dragon Crackers (see Appendices)

Freshly ground pepper

ENTRÉES

# Marinated Exotic Mushrooms with Kohlrabi and Arugula

*This preparation is earthy and to some extent hearty, but at the same time it is extremely delicate. The robust flavors of the mushrooms are balanced nicely by the kohlrabi, while the arugula, olive oil, and chopped herbs provide the final notes of refinement.*

**Method**—*To prepare the enoki mushrooms:* Whisk together the olive oil, lemon juice, shallot, and tarragon in a small bowl. Season to taste with salt and pepper. Place the enoki mushrooms in another bowl and pour the marinade over the top. Marinate for 1 hour.

*To prepare the black trumpet mushrooms:* Whisk together the truffle oil, lemon juice, and shallot in a small bowl. Season to taste with salt and pepper. Place the trumpet mushrooms in another bowl and pour the marinade over the top. Marinate for 1 hour.

*To prepare the golden chanterelle mushrooms:* Whisk together the olive oil, vinegar, and lemon juice in a small bowl. Season to taste with salt and pepper. Place the chanterelle mushrooms in another bowl and pour the marinade over the top. Marinate for 1 hour.

*To prepare the oyster mushrooms:* Whisk together the olive oil, vinegar, and lemon juice in a small bowl. Season to taste with salt and pepper. Place the oyster mushrooms in another bowl and pour the marinade over the top. Marinate for 1 hour.

*To prepare the kohlrabi:* Whisk together the olive oil, shoyu, water, garlic, and basil in a small bowl. Season to taste with salt and pepper. Place the kohlrabi in another bowl and pour the marinade over the top. Marinate for 1 hour.

*To prepare the arugula:* Combine the arugula and olive oil in a bowl and toss to coat the leaves evenly. Season to taste with salt and pepper.

**Assembly**—Remove all the marinated mushrooms and the kohlrabi from their marinades. Strain the marinades and then mix them together in a bowl. Arrange one-fourth of all the marinated mushrooms, the arugula, and the kohlrabi in a layered stack down the center of each plate. Spoon some of the reserved combined marinades on and around the mushrooms, making sure to use mainly the acid (lemon juice and vinegar) and only a little of the oil.

**Wine Notes**—The Piedmont region of Italy is known primarily for its red wines, but the Arneis is the star white varietal. Vigna Elisa from Paitin has notes of anise and minerals that intensify the flavors of the tarragon and arugula. It also has the body required for the full-textured nature of the chanterelle and oyster mushrooms.

## Serves 4

### Marinated Enoki Mushrooms

1/4 cup extra virgin olive oil

2 tablespoons freshly squeezed lemon juice

1 teaspoon minced shallot

1 teaspoon chopped fresh tarragon

Celtic sea salt and freshly ground pepper

1/4 pound enoki mushrooms

### Marinated Black Trumpet Mushrooms

2 tablespoons white truffle oil

2 tablespoons freshly squeezed lemon juice

1 teaspoon minced shallot

Celtic sea salt and freshly ground pepper

1/4 pound black trumpet mushrooms, pulled by hand into small pieces

### Marinated Golden Chanterelle Mushrooms

1/4 cup extra virgin olive oil

1 tablespoon balsamic vinegar

1 tablespoon freshly squeezed lemon juice

Celtic sea salt and freshly ground pepper

1/4 pound golden chanterelle mushrooms, cut into 1/4-inch pieces

### Marinated Oyster Mushrooms

1/4 cup extra virgin olive oil

1 tablespoon balsamic vinegar

1 tablespoon freshly squeezed lemon juice

Celtic sea salt and freshly ground pepper

1/4 pound oyster mushrooms, cut into 1/4-inch pieces

### Marinated Kohlrabi

2 tablespoons extra virgin olive oil

1 tablespoon nama shoyu

1 1/2 teaspoons filtered water

1/2 teaspoon minced garlic

1 teaspoon chopped fresh basil

Celtic sea salt and freshly ground pepper

1/4 pound kohlrabi, peeled and thinly sliced

### Arugula

2 ounces baby arugula

1 teaspoon extra virgin olive oil

Celtic sea salt and freshly ground pepper

# Stuffed Anaheim Chiles with Mole and Jicama and Baby Corn Salad

*The overall character of this dish is robust, yet the individual flavors are light and straightforward. Avocado, tiny corn, jicama, and pickled onion smoothly cut through the almost meaty filling of the chiles, and all of the flavors and textures are seamlessly woven together with the mole sauce.*

**Method**—*To make the stuffed chiles:* In a food processor, combine the walnuts, pine nuts, and cashews and process until smooth. Transfer to a bowl and stir in the barley miso, cilantro, scallion, basil, fresh corn kernels, tomato, cumin, jalapeño chile, garlic, oregano, lemon juice, chili powder, salt, and pepper to taste. Fill each chile with one-fourth of the nut mixture. (A pastry bag fitted with a small plain tip makes this task easier.) Place the chiles on a nonstick drying sheet on a dehydrator shelf and dehydrate at 105°F for 6 to 8 hours, or until tender but firm. Slice each chile on the diagonal into 5 equal slices.

*To make the mole:* The ancho and chipotle chiles are important here, but you can substitute other chiles for the others. Seed all the chiles, place them in a bowl with warm (105°F) filtered water to cover, and soak for 3 to 4 hours. Drain the chiles, rinse, drain again, and place in a high-speed blender. Add the almond butter, cinnamon stick, carrot juice, garlic, yellow onion, cilantro, dried corn kernels, raisins, tomato, cocoa powder, lime juice, cumin, cardamom, and Chocolate Sauce and process until smooth. Season to taste with salt and pepper.

*To make the Pickled Red Onions:* Combine all the ingredients in a glass jar with a tight-fitting lid and refrigerate for 1 week before using. Just before using, drain the onions and quarter them.

*To make the Jicama and Baby Corn Salad:* Combine the jicama, orange wedges, sliced baby corn, lime juice, and cilantro in a bowl and toss to mix. Season to taste with salt and pepper.

*To make the Cumin-Coriander Vinaigrette:* Combine the shallot, cumin, coriander, vinegar, and salt in a bowl. Slowly drizzle in the olive oil while whisking constantly. Season to taste with pepper.

**Assembly**—Spoon a ring of the mole on each plate. Drizzle the Sour Cream in a wavy line on the mole. Arrange 5 chile slices in a spoke pattern on the mole, and place some of the Jicama and Baby Corn Salad in the center of the plate, resting it on the chile slices. Sprinkle the red pearl onion wedges, diced avocado, and cilantro sprouts around the plate. Drizzle the vinaigrette around the plate and top with pepper.

**Wine Notes**—Thank goodness spicy foods have German Riesling to offset the heat! A Franz Kunstler Riesling Auslese from the Rheingau beautifully balances the Anaheim chiles and mole. The sharp acid backbone of Kunstler's wines do not mask the jicama or the corn salad, in spite of the great intensity of the wines.

## Serves 4

### Stuffed Chiles

1 cup raw walnuts, soaked for 10 to 12 hours in filtered water and drained

1 1/4 cups raw pine nuts, soaked for 4 to 6 hours in filtered water and drained

1/4 cup raw cashews, soaked for 10 to 12 hours in filtered water and drained

1 tablespoon barley miso

1/3 cup fresh cilantro leaves, chopped

1 tablespoon diced scallion, green and white parts

2 tablespoons minced fresh basil

3/4 cup fresh sweet corn kernels

1/4 cup diced, seeded tomato

1 teaspoon freshly ground cumin

1 teaspoon minced jalapeño chile

1 teaspoon minced garlic

1 teaspoon minced fresh oregano

1 1/2 teaspoons freshly squeezed lemon juice

1 teaspoon chili powder

1/2 teaspoon Celtic sea salt

Freshly ground pepper

4 red Anaheim chiles, stemmed and seeded

### Mole

1 ancho chile

1 chipotle chile

1 mirasol chile

2 guajillo chiles

1 pulla chile

2 pasilla chiles

1 tablespoon raw almond butter

1 small piece cinnamon stick

1/2 cup carrot juice

12 cloves garlic

1/2 cup chopped yellow onion

1 tablespoon fresh cilantro leaves

1 tablespoon dried sweet corn kernels

2 tablespoons raisins

1 large Roma tomato, cored and quartered lengthwise

2 tablespoons Green and Black's Organic cocoa powder

2 tablespoons freshly squeezed lime juice

1 teaspoon freshly ground cumin

1/8 teaspoon black cardamom seeds

5 tablespoons Chocolate Sauce (see Appendices)

Celtic sea salt and freshly ground pepper

### Pickled Red Onions

12 red pearl onions

1/4 cup red wine vinegar

1 teaspoon Celtic sea salt

2 turns of the pepper mill

## Jicama and Baby Corn Salad

³/₄ cup baton-cut, peeled jicama
(2 by ¹/₄-inch batons)

6 orange segments, supremed
and cut into tiny wedges

2 baby ears sweet corn,
thinly sliced

1 tablespoon freshly squeezed
lime juice

1 tablespoon chopped
fresh cilantro

Celtic sea salt and freshly
ground pepper

## Cumin-Coriander Vinaigrette

1 ¹/₂ teaspoons diced shallot

1 ¹/₂ teaspoons freshly
ground cumin

¹/₂ teaspoon freshly
ground coriander

2 tablespoons rice wine vinegar

¹/₄ teaspoon Celtic sea salt

¹/₄ cup extra virgin olive oil

Freshly ground pepper

## Garnish

¹/₄ cup Sour Cream
(see Appendices)

¹/₂ cup diced avocado

¹/₄ cup micro cilantro sprouts

Freshly ground pepper

STUFFED ANAHEIM CHILES WITH MOLE AND JICAMA
AND BABY CORN SALAD

# Tacos Three Ways with Mexican Vinaigrette

*These tacos can be combined and eaten as a main course, or they can be served individually as small appetizers. Each has its own character, but all of them shine with the addition of the vibrant and zesty Mexican Vinaigrette and the creamy and complex Sour Cream.*

**Method**—*To make the taco shells:* Combine the flaxseeds, sunflower seeds, and water in a bowl and refrigerate for 10 to 12 hours, or until all the liquid is absorbed. The next day, drain off any remaining liquid and transfer the seed mixture to a food processor. Add the Rejuvelac, onion, garlic powder, chili powder, cumin, and shoyu and blend until smooth, about 5 minutes. Add the poppy seeds and process to combine. Season to taste with salt and pepper.

Using an offset spatula, spread the seasoned seed mixture about $1/8$ inch thick onto 3 nonstick drying sheets. Place the sheets on dehydrator shelves and dehydrate at 105°F for 3 hours, or until the taco-shell sheet can be removed in a single piece. Slide the taco-shell sheets onto a work surface, cut out 12 rounds each 4 inches in diameter, and return the rounds to the nonstick drying sheets, flipping them over as you do. Dehydrate at 105°F for 1 hour, or until slightly firm. Remove from the dehydrator, fold up the sides of each round to create a taco shell, and return them to the dehydrator, placing them directly on the shelves. Continue to dehydrate at 105°F for 8 to 10 hours, or until crisp.

*To make the Mexican Red Chile Sauce:* In a high-speed blender, combine all the ingredients and process until smooth, adding a small amount of filtered water if needed to create a smooth consistency. Set aside $1/2$ cup of the sauce to use for the vinaigrette. Reserve the remainder for another use.

*To make the Mexican Vinaigrette:* In the high-speed blender, combine all the ingredients and process until smooth.

*To make the Guacamole:* Combine the avocado, onion, cilantro, lime juice, and salt in a bowl and stir to mix. Do not overmix; the texture should be slightly chunky. Season to taste with pepper. You should have about $1/2$ cup; set aside to use for making the filling for Taco No. 3.

*To make Taco No. 1:* Spread the black trumpet mushrooms and porcini on separate dehydrator shelves and dehydrate at 105°F for 2 hours, or until half-dried. Transfer the trumpets and porcini to a bowl, add the corn, lime juice, vinegar, olive oil, and cilantro, and toss to mix. Season to taste with salt. Spread the mixture on a nonstick drying sheet on a dehydrator shelf and dehydrate at 105°F for about 1 hour, or until softened. Divide the mixture evenly among 4 taco shells.

*To make Taco No. 2:* Combine the mustard green leaves, tomatoes, tomatillos, pear, onion, lime juice, and olive oil in a bowl and toss to mix. Season to taste with salt. Divide the mixture evenly among 4 taco shells, lining each shell with a mustard leaf.

*To make Taco No. 3:* Combine the mango, jicama, and lime juice in a bowl and toss to mix. Season to taste with salt. Divide the mango mixture and Guacamole evenly among 4 taco shells.

**Assembly**—Combine the Sour Cream and cilantro in a bowl and stir to mix. Soon some of the Sour Cream on the center of each plate, and spoon the vinaigrette in 3 pools around the sour cream. Spoon a touch of Sour Cream into the middle of each vinaigrette pool. Stand 1 taco upright in each pool, using a different type of taco for each pool and positioning the 3 tacos to form a triangle.

**Wine Notes**—The spicy aroma of Spain's Tempranillo grape harmonizes with all the tacos. This course is in the arena of red wine because of the weight and richness of the taco shells and because this is not an overtly piquant dish. With scents of cumin, coriander, and chiles, the Terreus from Bodegas Mauro accents all the earthy flavors of the trio.

Serves 4

### Taco Shells

3 cups golden flaxseed

1 cup raw sunflower seeds

3 cups filtered water

1 cup Rejuvelac (see Appendices)

2 tablespoons minced onion

2 teaspoons minced garlic

2 teaspoons chili powder

1 teaspoon freshly ground cumin

$^1/_3$ cup nama shoyu

2 tablespoons poppy seeds

Celtic sea salt and freshly
ground pepper

### Mexican Red Chile Sauce

$^3/_4$ cup chopped Roma tomato

1 $^1/_2$ ounces dried chiles,
including 2 pullas, 2 chilhuacles,
and 1 mild chipotle, seeded,
soaked for 30 minutes in warm
(105°F) filtered water, rinsed,
and drained

1 teaspoon finely chopped
fresh oregano

1 teaspoon minced garlic

1 teaspoon freshly ground cumin

1 teaspoon freshly squeezed
lemon juice

$^1/_2$ teaspoon apple cider vinegar

$^1/_8$ teaspoon smoked salt

$^1/_8$ teaspoon freshly
cracked pepper

1 $^1/_2$ teaspoons Date Paste
(see Appendices)

$^1/_2$ teaspoon Celtic sea salt

### Mexican Vinaigrette

Reserved $^1/_2$ cup Mexican Red
Chile Sauce

5 $^1/_2$ teaspoons white wine vinegar

1 teaspoon chili powder

$^1/_2$ teaspoon minced onion

$^1/_2$ cup extra virgin olive oil

4 teaspoons chopped fresh cilantro

$^1/_2$ teaspoon Date Paste
(see Appendices)

Scant $^1/_4$ teaspoon Celtic salt

Scant $^1/_2$ teaspoon diced
jalapeño chile

### Guacamole

$^1/_2$ avocado, peeled and diced

2 teaspoons minced white onion

2 $^1/_2$ teaspoons chopped
fresh cilantro

1 teaspoon freshly squeezed
lime juice

$^1/_4$ teaspoon Celtic sea salt

Freshly cracked pepper

### Taco No. 1

$^1/_3$ cup black trumpet mushrooms

$^1/_3$ cup sliced porcini mushrooms

$^3/_4$ cup sweet corn kernels

1 $^1/_2$ teaspoons freshly squeezed
lime juice

1 teaspoon chile vinegar

4 teaspoons extra virgin olive oil

6 fresh cilantro leaves, chopped

Celtic sea salt

### Taco No. 2

4 tiny mustard green leaves

$^1/_4$ cup brunoise-cut, seeded
red tomato

4 teaspoons julienned,
seeded red tomato

2 tomatillos, husks removed,
seeded, and cut into brunoise

$^1/_8$ Asian pear, peeled
and julienned

2 teaspoons minced red onion

1 teaspoon freshly squeezed
lime juice

2 teaspoons extra virgin olive oil

Celtic sea salt

### Taco No. 3

$^1/_4$ cup bruoise-cut,
peeled mango

$^1/_4$ cup brunoise-cut,
peeled jicama

2 teaspoons freshly squeezed
lime juice

Celtic sea salt

$^1/_2$ cup Guacamole

$^1/_2$ cup Sour Cream
(see Appendices)

1 tablespoon chopped
fresh cilantro

TACOS THREE WAYS WITH MEXICAN VINAIGRETTE

# Stuffed Squash Blossoms with Curried Parsnip Purée and Tobacco Onions

*This would be an ideal first course or appetizer for a special meal. The flavors are light and refreshing, and the curried parsnip provides just the right measure of richness. Crispy onion pieces add an important textural contrast, and the big flavors of the Indian spices are reinforced with the use of an infused oil that is drizzled on at the end.*

**Method**—*To make the Stuffed Squash Blossoms:* In a high-speed blender, combine the cashews, pine nuts, and parsnips and process until well mixed. Add the Almond Milk, olive oil, salt, onion, and spice mix and process until creamy. Season to taste with pepper. Spoon the filling into a pastry bag fitted with a large plain tip and pipe the filling into the squash blossoms.

*To make the Ratatouille:* Combine the zucchini, crookneck squashes, corn, onion, and olive oil in a bowl and stir gently to mix. Season to taste with salt and pepper. Spread the mixture on a dehydrator shelf and dehydrate at 105°F for 30 minutes, or until tender. Remove from the dehydrator and stir in the tomato, with any collected juices, and the basil. Taste and adjust the seasoning.

*To make the Tobacco Onions:* Combine the cracker crumbs, Rawmesan, basil, thyme, oregano, and cayenne in a bowl and stir to mix. Season to taste with salt and pepper. Lightly coat each onion ring with olive oil, then cover the rings with the crumb mixture, pressing the mixture onto rings with your fingertips so that it will adhere. Place the coated onion rings on a nonstick drying sheet on a dehydrator shelf and dehydrate at 105°F for 4 hours, or until dry to the touch.

*To make the Lime Vinaigrette:* Whisk together the olive oil, lime juice, chile, tomato, and cilantro in a bowl. Season to taste with salt and pepper.

**Assembly**—Spoon some of the Ratatouille onto each plate, positioning it slightly off center, and place a stuffed squash blossom at the center of the plate. Arrange some of the Tobacco Onions over the stem end of the squash blossom. Spoon 1 teaspoon Curry Oil and one-fourth of the Lime Vinaigrette around the plate. Sprinkle with 1 tablespoon of the cilantro sprouts.

**Wine Notes**—Josmeyer's Cuvée des Folastries is a medium-bodied Gewürztraminer that does not have a lot of sweetness, yet retains all of the flavor components that make Gewürztraminer famous. This wine accents the onion rings and curried parsnip purée especially well, while the ample flavor of the stuffing supports the zucchini and squash mixture, which would otherwise be overwhelmed.

Serves 4

## Stuffed Squash Blossoms

3/4 cup raw cashews, soaked for 10 to 12 hours in filtered water and drained

1/3 cup raw pine nuts

2 cups peeled, cored, and chopped parsnip

1/3 cup Almond Milk (see Appendices)

3 tablespoons extra virgin olive oil

1 teaspoon Celtic salt

1 1/2 teaspoons minced onion

4 teaspoons Indian Spice Mix (see Appendices)

Freshly ground pepper

4 squash blossoms

## Ratatouille

4 baby zucchini, cut crosswise into 1/8-inch-thick slices

4 baby crookneck squashes, cut crosswise into 1/8-inch-thick slices

Kernels from 1 ear sweet corn

2 tablespoons finely diced red onion

2 tablespoons extra virgin olive oil

Celtic sea salt and freshly ground pepper

1/2 cup diced, seeded tomato

1 tablespoon finely chiffonade-cut fresh Thai basil

## Tobacco Onions

1 cup Dragon Cracker crumbs (see Appendices)

1/2 cup Rawmesan (see Appendices)

2 tablespoons chopped fresh basil

1 tablespoon chopped fresh thyme

2 teaspoons chopped fresh oregano

1/4 teaspoon freshly ground cayenne pepper

Celtic sea salt and freshly ground pepper

1 cup thinly sliced red onion (1/8 inch thick), separated into rings

Extra virgin olive oil for coating

## Lime Vinaigrette

5 tablespoons olive oil

2 tablespoons freshly squeezed lime juice

1 tablespoon minced jalapeño chile

2 tablespoons brunoise-cut, seeded tomato

2 teaspoons chopped fresh cilantro

Celtic sea salt and freshly ground pepper

4 teaspoons Curry Oil (see Appendices)

4 tablespoons micro cilantro sprouts

# Curried Crepes with Yogurt Sauce

*The curry flavor ignites this preparation, yet it is successfully tamed by the Yogurt Sauce and the avocado. Apple and jicama contribute sweetness and the requisite crunch, while red and yellow tomatoes add a balancing acid and a pleasant meatiness. Festive notes come from lemon pieces, chopped herbs, a delicate tomato sauce, and a drizzle of Basil Oil. The result is a dish that you will want to savor slowly.*

**Method**—*To make the Curried Crepes:* In a high-speed blender, combine all the ingredients and process to form a smooth batter with the consistency of thick cream. For each crepe, using an offset spatula, spread 1/4 cup of the batter into an 8-inch round on a nonstick drying sheet. You should have 4 crepes in all. (Reserve any remaining batter for later use.) Place the sheets on dehydrator shelves and dehydrate at 105°F for 1 1/2 hours, or until pliable. Flip the crepes off the sheets onto the shelves and continue to dehydrate for 30 minutes longer, or until dry but still pliable.

*To make the Crepe Filling:* Combine the red and yellow tomatoes, apple, jicama, avocado, basil, and lemon juice in a bowl and toss to mix. Season to taste with salt and pepper.

*To make the Yogurt Sauce:* Combine all the ingredients in a bowl and stir to mix.

*To make the garnish:* Press the red tomato through a fine-mesh sieve into a bowl to form a thick pulp. Whisk in 1 tablespoon of the olive oil, and season to taste with salt and pepper. Press the yellow tomato through a fine-mesh sieve into a separate bowl to form a thick pulp. Whisk in the remaining 1 tablespoon olive oil and season to taste with salt and pepper

**Assembly**—Loosely fold each crepe into thirds, interweaving the filling in the folds, and place each crepe on a plate. Spoon one-fourth each of the Yogurt Sauce and the red and yellow tomato pulp garnishes around the plate. Sprinkle one-fourth each of the lemon pieces, thyme, basil, and rosemary around the plate and drizzle with 1 teaspoon of the Basil Oil.

**Wine Notes**—A wine with some residual sugar is usually necessary with curry because it tones down the spiciness. With this preparation, the Yogurt Sauce handles that cooling effect. Chalk Hill's Estate Vineyard Selection Pinot Gris, a dry version of the grape, is then able to complement the apple and jicama inside the crepes without being overshadowed by the curry flavors.

## Serves 4

### Curried Crepes

1 cup golden flax meal

1 cup chopped, skin-on Granny Smith apple

1/2 cup unsweetened shredded dried coconut

1 teaspoon curry paste

1/2 teaspoon freshly ground turmeric

1/2 teaspoon Celtic sea salt

1/2 teaspoon freshly ground cayenne pepper

1 tablespoon freshly squeezed lemon juice

2 cups filtered water

Celtic sea salt and freshly ground pepper

### Crepe Filling

1 small red tomato, peeled and julienned

1 small yellow tomato, peeled and julienned

1/2 Granny Smith apple, skin on, julienned

1/2 cup julienned jicama

1 avocado, peeled, pitted, and julienned

6 fresh basil leaves, chopped

1 tablespoon freshly squeezed lemon juice

Celtic sea salt and freshly ground pepper

### Yogurt Sauce

3/4 cup Sour Cream (see Appendices)

1 tablespoon freshly squeezed lemon juice

1 tablespoon grated lemon zest

### Garnish

1/2 cup chopped red tomato

2 tablespoons extra virgin olive oil

Celtic sea salt and freshly ground pepper

1/2 cup chopped yellow tomato

6 lemon segments, supremed and each cut into eighths

1 teaspoon fresh thyme leaves

1 tablespoon chopped fresh basil

1 teaspoon fresh young rosemary leaves

4 teaspoons Basil Oil (see Appendices)

# Dolmas with Dill–Sour Cream Sauce and Garlic Chips

*Grape leaves encase a mixture of parsnip and pine nut that is smooth and creamy. This appealing filling is further enhanced by the addition of garlic, lemon, and dried currants. A delicately spiced sour cream sauce is drizzled along the edge of the plate, while sweet yet pungent Garlic Chips are scattered around the dolmas.*

**Method**—*To make the filling:* Spread the minced onion on a nonstick drying sheet on a dehydrator shelf and dehydrate at 105°F for 20 minutes, or until slightly dry to the touch. In a food processor, pulse the parsnip until it forms ricelike pieces. Transfer the parsnip to a bowl. In a high-speed blender, combine the pine nuts, garlic, celery, and lemon juice and process until creamy. Add the mixture to the parsnip. Stir in the dehydrated onion, parsley, mint, salt, lemon zest, and currants.

*To make the dolmas:* Combine the olive oil, garlic, and lemon juice in a small bowl and mix well. Place 1 grape leaf, stem side up, on a work surface. Brush with some of the oil mixture. Place one-twelfth of the filling near the base of the leaf. Roll up like a cigar, tucking in the sides as you go. Make sure the roll is good and firm. Brush the roll with some of the oil mixture. Set aside. Repeat to make 12 rolls in all.

*To make the Dill–Sour Cream Sauce:* Combine the Sour Cream, lemon juice, olive oil, dill, mint, and chiles in a bowl and stir to combine. Season to taste with salt and pepper.

**Assembly**—Cut 4 of the dolmas in half on the diagonal. Trim the ends if necessary for them to stand upright. Spoon some of the Dill–Sour Cream Sauce around the plates and place 1 cut piece of the dolma at 12 o'clock and 1 cut piece at 4 o'clock. Lay 2 whole dolmas, overlapping them, in the center of the plate. Sprinkle with the Garlic Chips and marigold petals.

**Wine Notes**—The main flavors to contend with here are dill, lemon juice, and Sour Cream. Sauvignon Blanc is the perfect complement for the green tastes from the dill and the zing from the lemon juice, but the Dill–Sour Cream Sauce requires a fuller-bodied wine. A blend of Semillon and Sauvignon Blanc, a classic white Bordeaux cépage, will handle all of the elements. Chateau Talbot's Caillou Blanc or an Australian choice like Cullen's Cuvée Ephraim Clarke works beautifully with the dish.

## Serves 4

### Filling

1/2 cup minced onion

2 cups peeled, cored, and chopped parsnip

1/4 cup raw pine nuts

1 clove garlic

1/4 cup chopped celery

2 tablespoons freshly squeezed lemon juice

1/2 cup minced fresh parsley

1/4 cup firmly packed finely chopped fresh flat-leaf parsley

1/4 cup firmly packed finely chopped fresh mint

1 1/2 teaspoons Celtic sea salt

1/2 teaspoon grated lemon zest

1/3 cup dried currants, soaked for 1 hour in filtered water, drained, and patted dry

1/4 cup extra virgin olive oil

1 teaspoon minced garlic

2 teaspoons freshly squeezed lemon juice

12 brined grape leaves, soaked for 2 hours in filtered water, drained, and patted dry

### Dill–Sour Cream Sauce

2 cups Sour Cream (see Appendices)

1/4 cup freshly squeezed lemon juice

1/4 cup extra virgin olive oil

1/2 cup chopped fresh dill

1/4 cup chopped fresh mint

2 serrano chiles, minced

Celtic sea salt and freshly ground pepper

4 teaspoons Garlic Chips (see Appendices)

4 teaspoons chopped marigold petals

# Lasagna

*Everything about this dish is light, clean, vibrant, and harmonious, with the wonderful taste of corn perhaps taking center stage. The corn's refined sweetness is marvelously juxtaposed with the elegant sour flavor in the cheese. Mushrooms provide an earthiness, and spinach leaves cut through all the elements to ensure a clean, bright taste. A playful salad featuring buttery lettuces, tomato pieces, and Rawmesan adds even greater depth on the palate. Here, both the flavor and the textural variety are extraordinary.*

**Method**—*To make the Marinara Sauce:* In a food processor, pulse the sun-dried tomatoes until reduced to small pieces. Add the Roma tomatoes, cherry tomatoes, garlic, salt, shallot, olive oil, maple syrup, and lemon juice and process until smooth. Add the basil, oregano, and thyme and pulse for about 4 minutes, or until the herbs are chopped.

Combine the corn and onion, spread on a dehydrator shelf, and dehydrate at 105°F for 1 hour, or until softened. (This brief drying helps to reduce the harsh flavor of the vegetables.) Set aside until needed.

Combine the mushrooms, shoyu, garlic, and 2 tablespoons of the olive oil in a bowl and let stand for 20 minutes. Drain, cover, and set aside until needed.

Using a mandoline, cut the zucchini lengthwise into wide, paper-thin slices. Set aside until needed.

Just before assembling the lasagna, combine the spinach, basil, a pinch of salt, and the remaining 2 tablespoons olive oil in a bowl and toss to mix.

*To assemble the lasagna:* Line a 7 by 3 by 3-inch metal terrine mold with detachable sides with plastic wrap, allowing an overhang on the long sides. Arrange a layer of the zucchini "noodles" in the terrine, covering the bottom and the sides and allowing the noodles to overhang the rim by 2 inches. Layer on top, in the following order: a double layer of mushrooms; half of the Herb Cheese; a layer of spinach 3 leaves deep; half of the Marinara Sauce; half of the corn and onion; a sprinkle of salt and pepper; a double layer of zucchini noodles, one running horizontally and one running vertically; the remaining mushrooms in 2 layers, the remaining Herb Cheese, a layer of spinach 3 leaves deep, the remaining Marinara Sauce, the remaining corn and onion, a sprinkle of salt and pepper, and the remaining spinach leaves in 1 layer. Pull up on the plastic wrap to tighten the sides, then fold over the overhanging pieces of zucchini. Patch with more zucchini as needed to cover fully with a zucchini layer. Cover with the overhanging plastic wrap and press down firmly. Refrigerate for 3 hours. Detach the mold sides, remove the plastic-wrapped terrine from the mold, and tighten the plastic wrap by pulling a long edge taut. With the plastic wrap still in place, cut the terrine into 8 slices each a scant 1 inch thick. Carefully remove the plastic wrap from each slice. The layers may shift slightly, but you can easily push them back together.

*To make the Corn Sauce:* In a high-speed blender, combine the corn, olive oil, and water and purée until smooth. Pass through a fine-mesh sieve and season to taste with salt and pepper.

*To make the salad:* Combine the tomatoes, lettuces, Rawmesan, lemon juice, and olive oil in a bowl and toss to mix. Season to taste with salt and pepper.

**Assembly**—Place a slice of the terrine just below the center of each plate. Arrange one-fourth of the salad at 12 o'clock. Spoon one-fourth of the Corn Sauce to the right of the terrine slice and drizzle 2 teaspoons Basil Oil over the Corn Sauce. Top with pepper.

**Wine Notes**—Although my mom's lasagna was quite different, the wine that my parents always drank with it is perfect for this dish. Fruitier, fuller-bodied Barberas from the modern school are the choice here because the Corn Sauce and cheese would mask the lighter body and lack of fruit intensity of a traditional Barbera. Producers such as Roberto Voerzio and Prunotto are highly recommended.

Serves 4

### Marinara Sauce

2 cups dry-packed sun-dried
tomatoes, soaked for 1 to 4 hours
in filtered water and drained

4 Roma tomatoes, halved
and seeded

12 cherry tomatoes,
or 3 additional Roma tomatoes,
halved and seeded

4 cloves garlic

$1/2$ teaspoon Celtic salt

1 tablespoon chopped shallot

3 tablespoons extra virgin olive oil

2 tablespoons maple syrup

$1/2$ teaspoon freshly squeezed
lemon juice

8 fresh basil leaves

2 tablespoons fresh
oregano leaves

$1 1/2$ teaspoons fresh
thyme leaves

1 cup sweet corn kernels

$1/4$ cup minced onion

4 cups cremini mushrooms,
sliced $1/8$ inch thick

2 tablespoons nama shoyu

$2 1/2$ cloves garlic, smashed

4 tablespoons extra virgin olive oil

4 zucchini, each 8 to
10 inches long and $1 1/2$ inches
in diameter

1 bunch spinach, stems removed

$1/2$ cup fresh basil leaves,
cut into chiffonade

Celtic sea salt and freshly
ground pepper

$1 1/4$ cups Herb Cheese
(see Appendices)

### Corn Sauce

$1/2$ cup sweet corn kernels

$1/4$ cup extra virgin olive oil

$1/4$ cup filtered water

Celtic sea salt and freshly
ground pepper

### Salad

20 grape tomatoes, halved

3 cups tiny lettuces

6 tablespoons shaved Rawmesan
(see Appendices)

2 teaspoons freshly squeezed
lemon juice

4 teaspoons extra virgin olive oil

Celtic sea salt and freshly
ground pepper

8 teaspoons Basil Oil
(see Appendices)

Freshly ground pepper

LASAGNA

# Bleeding Heart Radish Ravioli with Yellow Tomato Sauce

*This stunning preparation, which can be adjusted for serving as an appetizer or a main dish, is actually quite simple to make. The herbed cheese filling melts away to a divine creaminess that is balanced by the mild, barely crunchy radish pieces. Diced yellow tomatoes, marinated in olive oil, act as the sauce and provide a complementary acidic note. For a different textural effect, process the tomato sauce in a high-speed blender.*

**Method**—*To make the ravioli:* Use a 2-inch ring mold to cut each radish slice into a perfect round. Rub the radish slices with the olive oil and lemon juice and season with salt. Place 1 tablespoon of the cheese in the center of half of the radish slices. Carefully place a second radish slice on top of the spoonful of cheese and gently press the outer edges together to create a seal. Repeat to make 20 ravioli in all.

Combine the tomatoes, chives, olive oil, and vinegar in a bowl and mix gently. Season to taste with salt and pepper.

**Assembly**—Using a slotted spoon, spoon one-fourth of the tomato mixture into the center of each plate. Arrange 5 ravioli over the tomatoes, overlapping them slightly. Spoon some of the juices from the tomatoes on top. Sprinkle with the basil flowers.

**Wine Notes**—There are a number of good possibilities here. Sangiovese springs to mind when tasting this dish because it is one of the few red wines that is not flabby when paired with the racy acidity of tomatoes. Isole e Olena Chianti is a light-bodied, fruity red that slices nicely through the richness of the herbed cheese. During peak season, when tomatoes are at their sweetest and ripest, a Barbera from Vietti or Dolcetto d'Alba from Pio Cesare would be a magical choice.

## Serves 4

### Ravioli

40 very thin slices peeled bleeding heart radish, each at least 2 1/4 inches in diameter

2 tablespoons extra virgin olive oil

1 tablespoon freshly squeezed lemon juice

Celtic sea salt

1 1/4 cups Herb Cheese (see Appendices)

2 large, very ripe yellow tomatoes, seeded and cut into medium dice

2 1/2 tablespoons chopped fresh chives

1/2 cup extra virgin olive oil

1 teaspoon sherry wine vinegar

Celtic sea salt and freshly ground pepper

2 teaspoons fresh opal basil flowers or micro leaves

# Young Coconut Pad Thai with Almond Chile Sauce

*The young coconut pieces have a texture almost identical to that of the noodles in traditional pad Thai. The cashews, cabbage, apple, and carrot provide refreshing flavors and a delightful textural counterpoint to the soft coconut. A beautifully complex chile sauce adds just the right creaminess, and serrano chile pieces deliver the perfect refined heat. This glorious preparation will be the star at any dinner party.*

**Method**—*To make the Tamarind Juice:* Split open the tamarind pods and discard the pods. Place the pulp-covered seeds in filtered water to cover and let soak for 1 hour. Drain and, using your fingers, remove the pulp that surrounds the seeds; discard the seeds. Place the pulp in a small bowl and whisk in just enough filtered water to create a smooth, medium-bodied mixture. Measure out 2 tablespoons; reserve the remainder for another use.

*To make the Pad Thai:* In a high-speed blender, combine the Tamarind Juice, maple syrup, shoyu, garlic, minced serrano chile, olive oil, and salt and process until smooth. Place the zucchini, cabbage, carrot, onion, apple, bell pepper, coconut meat, sliced serrano chile, and cilantro in a bowl. Add the tamarind purée and toss to coat. Season the mixture to taste with salt and pepper.

*To make the Almond Chile Sauce:* In the high-speed blender, combine the almond butter, ginger, garlic, Thai dragon chile, lemon juice, maple syrup, and shoyu and process until smooth, adding the water to thin if necessary. The sauce should have the consistency of melted ice cream. Season to taste with salt and pepper.

**Assembly**—Arrange some of the Pad Thai mixture in the center of each plate. Spoon one-fourth of the Almond Chile Sauce, 1 teaspoon of the shoyu, and $1/2$ teaspoon of the sesame oil around the Pad Thai. Sprinkle with the cashews.

**Wine Notes**—Classic Asian flavors always seem to call for Riesling because the elegant grape is able to showcase all of the spices. With the multitude of flavors in the Pad Thai, including a tart tamarind sauce, apples, and cilantro, a German Kabinett is a solid direction. Studert-Prum and Dr. Thanisch both produce invigorating styles that interweave with the myriad flavors. Their wines also retain a hint of sweetness that quells any concerns over the serrano chiles dominating the dish.

## Serves 4

### Tamarind Juice

2 tamarind pods

Filtered water as needed

### Pad Thai

2 tablespoons Tamarind Juice

$1 1/2$ tablespoons maple syrup

$1 1/2$ tablespoons nama shoyu

$1 1/2$ teaspoons minced garlic

$1 1/4$ teaspoons minced serrano chile

1 tablespoon extra virgin olive oil

$1/4$ teaspoon Celtic sea salt

1 cup julienned zucchini

1 cup finely shredded red cabbage

1 cup julienned carrot

$1/2$ cup julienned red onion

1 cup julienned, skin-on Granny Smith apple

$1/2$ cup julienned red bell pepper

3 cups julienned young Thai coconut meat

1 serrano chile, thinly sliced

2 tablespoons fresh cilantro leaves

Celtic sea salt and freshly ground pepper

### Almond Chile Sauce

$1/2$ cup raw almond butter

1 tablespoon minced, peeled fresh ginger

2 cloves garlic

1 Thai dragon chile

2 tablespoons freshly squeezed lemon juice

2 tablespoons maple syrup

1 tablespoon nama shoyu

$1/4$ cup filtered water, if need to thin

Celtic sea salt and freshly ground pepper

4 teaspoons nama shoyu

2 teaspoons cold-pressed sesame oil

$1/4$ cup Spicy Cashews (see Appendices)

# Polenta with Wild Mushroom Ragout

*The polenta has a creamy texture and refined corn flavor. The mushroom ragout, which is spooned over the top, helps to make the dish even lustier. Finally, a tasty mushroom purée and a bit of truffle oil are drizzled around the plate to provide a satiny richness. In all, this is a splendid combination of flavors and textures.*

**Method**—*To make the polenta:* In a high-speed blender, combine 1 1/2 cups of the corn, the pine nuts, cashews, onion, chile, garlic, salt, lemon juice, black pepper, and cayenne and process until the mixture resembles wet cornmeal. Transfer to a bowl and stir in the remaining corn and the cilantro. Divide among four 3-inch ring molds on a dehydrator shelf. Dehydrate at 105°F for 4 hours, or until a dry crust forms on the top of each mold.

*To make the Wild Mushroom Ragout:* Combine all the mushrooms, the olive oil, lemon juice, celery, and shallot in a bowl and toss to mix. Season to taste with salt and pepper. Cover, place on a dehydrator shelf, and dehydrate at 105°F for 1 1/2 hours, or until the mushrooms look like they are cooked. Fold in the parsley, thyme, and truffle oil. Taste and adjust the seasoning.

*To make the Mushroom Bouillon:* In a food processor, combine the mushrooms, carrot, celery, onion, and leek, and pulse until all the vegetables are the size of rice kernels. Transfer to a bowl and stir in the thyme, tarragon, and parsley. Spread in a thin layer on a nonstick drying sheet on a dehydrator shelf and dehydrate at 105°F for 4 hours, or until completely dry and crisp. Remove from the dehydrator and grind to a powder in a spice grinder. Return the powder to a bowl and stir in the olive oil and salt. Measure out 2 teaspoons to use for making the broth and sauce. Reserve the remainder for another use.

*To make the Mushroom Broth:* Combine the bouillon and water and stir to combine. Season to taste with salt and pepper.

*To make the Mushroom Sauce:* In the high-speed blender, combine all the ingredients and process until smooth. Taste and adjust the seasoning with salt and pepper. Measure out 1/2 cup; reserve the remainder for another use (only a small amount will remain).

**Assembly**—Using a spoon, scoop out a large spoonful of polenta from each mold, including the creamy portion and the crisp top in each spoonful, and place in the center of a plate. Top with one-fourth of the ragout. Spoon 1 tablespoon of the broth, 2 tablespoons of the sauce, and 1 1/2 teaspoons of the truffle oil around the polenta.

**Wine Notes**—Oregon Pinot Noirs offer the best of both worlds. They are a hybrid of the fruit and power of California and the earthiness and bright acidity of Burgundy. Brickhouse's Pinot pairs nicely with the contrasting elements—the woodsy nature of the mushrooms and the hint of sweetness of the polenta—present in the dish.

## Serves 4

### Polenta

2 1/2 cups sweet corn kernels

1/4 cup raw pine nuts

1/4 cup raw cashews, soaked for 10 to 12 hours in filtered water and drained

1 tablespoon finely diced onion

2 1/2 teaspoons finely diced jalapeño chile

1 teaspoon minced garlic

3/4 teaspoon Celtic sea salt

1/8 teaspoon freshly squeezed lemon juice

1/8 teaspoon freshly ground black pepper

Pinch of freshly ground cayenne pepper

2 tablespoons chopped fresh cilantro

### Wild Mushroom Ragout

1 ounce lobster mushrooms

1 ounce pom pom mushrooms

2 ounces shiitake mushrooms

1 ounce cinnamon cap mushrooms

1/4 cup extra virgin olive oil

1 teaspoon freshly squeezed lemon juice

2 tablespoons finely diced celery

1 tablespoon finely diced shallot

Celtic sea salt and freshly ground pepper

1 tablespoon minced fresh flat-leaf parsley

1/2 teaspoon chopped fresh thyme

2 teaspoons black truffle oil

### Mushroom Bouillon

2 1/2 ounces portobello mushrooms, cut into 1/2-inch pieces

1 1/2 teaspoons diced carrot

1 1/2 teaspoons diced celery

1 tablespoon diced onion

1 tablespoon diced leek, white part only

1/8 teaspoon chopped fresh thyme

1/8 teaspoon chopped fresh tarragon

1/8 teaspoon chopped fresh flat-leaf parsley

1 1/2 teaspoons extra virgin olive oil

Scant 1/2 teaspoon Celtic sea salt

### Mushroom Broth

1 teaspoon Mushroom Bouillon

1/4 cup warm (105°F) filtered water

Celtic sea salt and freshly ground pepper

### Mushroom Sauce

1 cup chopped portobello mushrooms

1/2 cup filtered water

1 tablespoon extra virgin olive oil

1 1/2 teaspoons tarragon wine vinegar

1/4 teaspoon chopped garlic

1/4 teaspoon Celtic sea salt

1 tablespoon Mushroom Bouillon

1/8 teaspoon freshly cracked pepper

2 tablespoons black truffle oil

# Portobello Mushroom Pavé with White Asparagus Vinaigrette

*The meatiness of the marinated portobellos is enormously satisfying, but the aromatic flavor notes delivered by the jalapeño, garlic, and ginger, along with the cilantro and soy, are what push this creation over the top. The creamy white asparagus contributes richness and acts as the perfect cohesive element. Button or cremini mushrooms would be suitable substitutes for the portobellos.*

**Method**—*To make the pavé:* Remove the stems and gills from the mushrooms. Discard the stems and place the gills in a bowl. Add the water and let stand while you slice the mushrooms. Cut the mushrooms on the extreme diagonal into paper-thin slices.

Combine the shoyu, ginger, garlic, chile, cilantro, shallot, and lemon juice in a bowl. Strain the liquid from the mushroom trimmings, discarding the solids, and add the liquid to the shoyu mixture. Carefully dip each mushroom slice into the shoyu mixture and lay the slices in the bottom of a shallow container. Pour the remaining shoyu mixture over them. Cover with plastic wrap and refrigerate for 2 hours.

Line a 4 by 4 by 2-inch pan with plastic wrap, allowing an overhang on 2 opposite sides. Remove the mushrooms slices from the liquid and layer them in the prepared pan, overlapping the slices and continuing until you have used all the slices. Cover with the overhanging plastic wrap and press down gently with your hand. Top with another pan that fits inside the rim, then place a 2-pound weight on the second pan. Refrigerate the pavé for at least 2 hours or up to overnight.

Just before serving, remove the weight and the second pan, then invert the pavé onto a cutting board and peel away the plastic wrap. Cut into 4 equal pieces, reserving any juices that drip from the pavé.

*To make the White Asparagus Vinaigrette:* Slice the white asparagus into ¼-inch-long pieces. Combine the asparagus pieces and mint in a bowl and toss to mix. In a high-speed blender, combine the grapeseed oil, vinegar, lemon juice, tahini, sesame seeds, shallot, garlic, coriander, and water and process until smooth. Pass the purée through a fine-mesh sieve placed over a bowl. Fold in the asparagus mixture and season to taste with salt and pepper. Measure out 8 tablespoons; reserve the remainder for another use.

**Assembly**—Place a piece of the pavé in the center of each plate. Spoon the reserved juices from the pavé around the plate. Drizzle 2 tablespoons of the asparagus vinaigrette around the plate and top with pepper.

**Wine Notes**—Pisoni Estate Pinot Noir offers an exciting contrast to the earthy flavor of the portobellos. Located in the Santa Lucia Highlands of California's Monterey County, Pisoni's estate vineyard is planted with ungrafted Pinot Noir vines that produce wines of incredible fruit intensity and richness. These deftly balanced wines will also elevate the soy and sesame flavors of the dish.

## Serves 4

### Pavé

6 large portobello mushrooms

2 ½ cups filtered water

½ cup nama shoyu

¼ cup minced, peeled fresh ginger

1 teaspoon minced garlic

1 jalapeño chile, seeded and minced

¼ cup chopped fresh cilantro

¼ cup minced shallot

2 tablespoons freshly squeezed lemon juice

### White Asparagus Vinaigrette

2 stalks pencil-thin white asparagus, trimmed

1 ½ teaspoons chopped fresh mint

2 tablespoons grapeseed oil

1 tablespoon rice wine vinegar

1 tablespoon freshly squeezed lemon juice

2 tablespoons raw tahini

½ cup plus 1 ½ teaspoons white sesame seeds

1 tablespoon minced shallot

½ teaspoon minced garlic

¼ teaspoon freshly ground coriander

½ cup plus 2 tablespoons filtered water

Celtic sea salt and freshly ground pepper

Freshly ground pepper

DESSERTS

# Watermelon Soup with Sharlyn Melon Granité and Micro Mint

*Although this soup is light and delicate, it promises a bounty of flavor. A mound of Sharlyn melon granité rests on a salad of cubed watermelon, Sharlyn melon, and jicama, resulting in a true celebration of melon. These distinctive flavors and textures mingle nicely and are given a final flavor boost with the additions of micro mint and pepper.*

**Method**—*To make the granité:* In a food processor, purée the chopped Sharlyn melon until it is a thick liquid. Pass the purée through a fine-mesh sieve lined with clean cheesecloth placed over a bowl, reserving the pulp and juice separately. Pour the juice into a shallow pan and place in the freezer. After 30 minutes, remove the pan from the freezer and stir the juice with a spoon. Repeat until the juice begins to harden, about 1 hour. Then, every 20 minutes, scrape the granité with a spoon, creating a snowlike result, until it is set, 10 to 12 hours total.

*To make the soup:* In a high-speed blender, process the chopped watermelon until it is a medium-bodied liquid. Pass the purée through a fine-mesh sieve lined with cheesecloth placed over a bowl and discard the pulp.

*To make the salad:* Combine all the ingredients in a bowl and toss to mix.

**Assembly**—Using a ring mold 3 inches in diameter and 2 inches deep, arrange one-fourth of the salad in the center of each shallow bowl, then carefully lift off the mold. Ladle one-fourth of the soup around the salad. Arrange the reserved Sharlyn melon pulp at 6 points around the salad. Scrape the granité and arrange one-fourth of it on top of the salad. Sprinkle with 1 teaspoon of the mint and top with pepper.

**Wine Notes**—This combination has a subtle sweetness that should not be masked by a heavy, intense dessert wine. A demi-sec Champagne with its faint sweetness and cleansing effervescence is an exceptional companion to this course. Veuve Clicquot Ponsardin produces an elegant demi-sec that will showcase the melon flavors of the soup and the granité

Serves 4

**Granité**

3 cups chopped Sharlyn melon

**Soup**

4 cups chopped red watermelon

**Salad**

1/2 cup 1/4-inch-dice jicama

1/2 cup 1/4-inch-dice Sharlyn melon

1/2 cup 1/4-inch-dice red watermelon

1/2 cup 1/4-inch-dice watermelon rind, outer green layer removed

2 tablespoons freshly squeezed lime juice

1 tablespoon grated lime zest

4 teaspoons fresh micro mint leaves

Freshly ground pepper

# Kabocha Squash Soup with Sweet-and-Sour Sultana Sorbet

*The natural sweetness of the satiny kabocha squash soup is ably tamed by the Sultana Sorbet. Thin strands of dehydrated ginger provide an additional bite, and pepitas add an important textural note. Although the individual flavors are simple, they become dazzlingly complex when combined.*

**Method**—*To make the soup:* Arrange the squash slices on a dehydrator shelf and dehydrate at 105°F for 16 hours, or until dry. Remove from the dehydrator and soak in the water for 6 hours.

Combine the julienned squash with 1 tablespoon of the maple syrup in a bowl and toss to coat the squash evenly. Spread on a nonstick drying sheet on a dehydrator shelf and dehydrate at 105°F for 4 hours, or until dry. Combine the ginger and 1 tablespoon of the maple syrup in a bowl and toss to mix. Sprinkle to taste with salt. Spread on a nonstick drying sheet on a dehydrator shelf and dehydrate at 105°F for 4 hours, or until dry. Spread the pepitas on a dehydrator shelf and dehydrate at 105°F for 8 hours, or until dry.

In a high-speed blender, combine the kabocha slices and their water, the remaining 1 tablespoon maple syrup, 1 teaspoon of the dried julienned ginger, and 1 tablespoon of the dried julienned kabocha and process until smooth. Taste and adjust the sweetness with maple syrup if needed. Pass through a fine-mesh sieve.

*To make the Sultana Sorbet:* In the high-speed blender, combine the sultanas and their soaking water, the vinegar, and the nutmeg and purée until smooth. Pass the purée through a fine-mesh sieve. Freeze in an ice-cream maker according to the manufacturer's directions.

**Assembly**—Divide the soup evenly among shallow bowls. Sprinkle the remaining julienned squash and julienned ginger and the pepitas around the soup. Place a quenelle of the sorbet in the center of each bowl.

**Wine Notes**—The soup itself does not require a full-bodied wine, but the creaminess of the sorbet adds another layer to the dish that must be matched. An off-dry Viognier from Garretson, the Chumhra rises to the occasion. Its floral and candied-ginger aromas emphasize the ginger flavors in the soup without overwhelming the subtleness of the squash.

## Serves 4

### Soup

1 pound kabocha squash, peeled and sliced 1/4 inch thick

3 cups filtered water

1/4 cup finely julienned, peeled kabocha squash

3 tablespoons maple syrup, or as needed

1/4 cup finely julienned, peeled fresh ginger, soaked for 3 hours in filtered water and drained

Celtic sea salt

1/4 cup pepitas, soaked for 8 to 10 hours in filtered water and drained

### Sultana Sorbet

2 cups sultanas, soaked for 1 hour in 1 cup filtered water

1 1/2 teaspoons rice wine vinegar

1/8 teaspoon freshly grated nutmeg

# Tropical Fruit Spring Rolls
## with Coconut Sorbet

*Here, a thin sheet of pineapple encloses tropical fruits and chopped macadamias to create a spring roll of sorts. The united flavors and textures are succulent and clean, and the presentation announces that pure elegance has arrived. The heavenly Coconut Sorbet adds to the beautifully exotic flavors of the tropical fruits. Passion fruit and hojosanta provide the final flavor notes to what is already an enchanting combination. Serve a smaller version as a predessert, or even offer the regular portion as a lunchtime main course on a warm summer day.*

**Method**—Peel the pineapple. Cut a 4-inch-long section of the pineapple. Using an electric slicer or a large, sharp knife, cut the section length-wise to yield paper-thin slices, keeping them as large as possible and being careful not to cut into the core. Arrange the slices into four 6-inch squares, overlapping the slices slightly as necessary and trimming the edges if needed to make them even. Core and chop enough of the remaining pineapple to measure 3 cups and set aside for making the Pineapple Emulsion.

*To make the filling:* Using a high-speed blender, process the chopped coconut meat until smooth. Place in a bowl and add the julienned coconut, kiwifruits, mamey sapote, macadamia nuts, and longans. Stir gently to combine.

*To make the spring rolls:* Place a 6-inch pineapple square on a sheet of plastic wrap. Place one-fourth of the filling along the base of the pineapple square and roll up the square like a cigar, pulling away the plastic wrap as you roll. Wrap the finished roll tightly in the plastic wrap and refrigerate for 30 minutes. Repeat with the remaining pineapple squares and filling. Trim the rough edges off both ends of each spring roll, and then cut each roll in half on the diagonal. Remove the plastic wrap.

*To make the Coconut Sorbet:* In the high-speed blender, combine the coconut water and meat and the honey granules and process until smooth. Pass the purée through a fine-mesh sieve and freeze in an ice-cream maker according to the manufacturer's directions. You will have more than you need for this recipe; reserve the remainder for another use.

*To make the Pineapple Emulsion:* In the high-speed blender, combine the chopped pineapple and water and process at high speed for about 3 minutes. Pour into a deep, narrow container and let stand for 10 minutes, or until a layer of froth forms on top.

*To make the Coconut Emulsion:* Just before serving, pour the coconut milk into a deep bowl. Using an immersion blender, blend the coconut milk until a light froth forms on top.

**Assembly**—Place 2 spring roll halves in the center of each plate, standing them upright. Spoon the passion fruit pulp and seeds on and around the spring rolls. Place a quenelle each of the Pineapple Emulsion and the Coconut Sorbet at opposite points around the spring rolls. Spoon some of the Coconut Emulsion around the plate. Sprinkle with the hojasanta chiffonade and longan pieces.

**Wine Notes**—This dish is all about tropical flavors and summertime, and the last thing you want to do is overwhelm those delicate notes. A glass of Moscato d'Asti, the soda pop of wines, nicely accompanies the spring rolls, its ripe fruitiness and refreshing bubbles enlivening all of the flavors. If you are looking for a more serious wine, try a Riesling Auslese from Josef Biffar, which has the sweetness and zippy acidity to match the lip-smacking tartness of the pineapple and passion fruit.

**Serves 4**

1 pineapple

**Filling**

1 cup chopped young Thai
coconut meat

$1/2$ cup julienned young
Thai coconut meat

2 kiwifruits, peeled and cut
into batons

$1/2$ cup baton-cut mamey sapote

$1/3$ cup coarsely chopped raw
macadamia nuts

8 longans, peeled, pitted,
and coarsely chopped

**Coconut Sorbet**

Water and meat from 1 young
Thai coconut

3 tablespoons honey granules,
or to taste

**Pineapple Emulsion**

3 cups chopped pineapple

$1/4$ cup filtered water

**Coconut Emulsion**

2 cups fresh coconut milk

1 passion fruit, halved and seeds
and pulp scooped out

4 teaspoons fresh hojasanta
leaves. cut into fine chiffonade

6 longans, peeled, pitted,
and quartered

TROPICAL FRUIT SPRING ROLLS WITH COCONUT SORBET

# Indian Red Peaches with Vanilla Ice Cream and Pecan Praline

*This dish is simple yet exquisite, and the flavors are deeply satisfying. Dehydrating the peach slices slightly concentrates their flavor. The ice cream gains its sweetness from maple syrup; when combined with pecan and vanilla, the result is a gloriously haunting flavor. Chunks of praline provide a splendid crunchy texture, and small tarragon leaves bring a peppery note. The final strength of the preparation comes from the fact that it is not overly sweet.*

**Method**—*To make the Pecan Praline:* Combine all the ingredients in a bowl and mix well. Spread the mixture on a nonstick drying sheet on a dehydrator shelf and dehydrate at 105°F for 12 hours, or until crisp. Break the praline into small pieces.

*To make the Vanilla Ice Cream:* In a high-speed blender, combine the coconut water, Almond Milk, coconut meat, coconut oil, maple syrup, date sugar, and vanilla seeds, and process until smooth. Transfer to a bowl and fold in the Pecan Praline. Freeze in an ice-cream maker according to the manufacturer's directions. You will have more than you need for this recipe; reserve the remainder for another use.

Place the peaches in a bowl. In a small bowl, stir the vanilla seeds into the maple syrup, then drizzle the mixture over the peaches. Toss to coat. Place the peaches on a nonstick drying sheet on a dehydrator shelf and dehydrate at 105°F for 20 minutes, or until softened. Reserve any juices that remain in the bowl for garnishing the plates.

**Assembly**—Arrange one-fourth of the peach pieces in the center of each plate. Spoon the reserved juices from the peaches around the plate, and then sprinkle the Pecan Praline and tarragon around the plate. Place a quenelle of the Vanilla Ice Cream over the peaches.

**Wine Notes**—The flavor of the peaches is concentrated, which requires an overtly peachy, syrupy dessert wine. The praline also demands a full-bodied, viscous wine. Late-harvest New World Rieslings, such as Trefethen from the Napa Valley and Mount Horrock's Cordon Cut from the Clare Valley of Australia, are dominating wines that increase the hedonistic pleasures of the dish

**Serves 4**

### Pecan Praline

1 cup raw pecans, soaked for 10 to 12 hours in filtered water, rinsed, and drained

6 tablespoons maple syrup

1/8 teaspoon freshly grated nutmeg

3/4 teaspoon freshly ground cinnamon

1/8 teaspoon Celtic sea salt

### Vanilla Ice Cream

1 cup coconut water

1 1/2 cups Almond Milk (see Appendices)

3/4 cup chopped young Thai coconut meat

2 tablespoons coconut oil

1/4 cup maple syrup

1/4 cup date sugar

Seeds from 1/4 vanilla bean

1/2 cup Pecan Praline pieces

4 Indian Red peaches, pitted and cut lengthwise into eighths

Seeds from 1 vanilla bean

1/4 cup maple syrup

1/2 cup Pecan Praline pieces

4 teaspoons fresh micro tarragon leaves

# Fig Napoleon with Honey Pastry Cream and Basil

*The flavors and textures in this dish are both sensual and soul satisfying. The figs almost melt into the pastry cream, and both are beautifully offset by the crunchy baklava tuile pieces. Torn basil leaves add a necessary contrasting flavor note, providing a clean, peppery playfulness. Peaches or fraises de bois are good substitutions for the figs.*

**Method**—*To make the Baklava Tuiles:* In a food processor, combine all the ingredients and process until very smooth. Using an offset spatula, spread the mixture onto nonstick drying sheets, forming two 10-inch squares and making them as thin as possible. Place the sheets on dehydrator shelves and dehydrate at 105°F for 3 to 4 hours, or until firm enough to handle. Flip the tuile sheets onto the dehydrator shelves and, using a pizza wheel, score each sheet into 8 squares of equal size. Continue to dehydrate at 105°F until crisp. This will take about 24 hours.

*To make the Honey Pastry Cream:* In a high-speed blender, combine all the ingredients and process until the mixture has the consistency of a thick, velvety cream.

*To make the Fig Sauce:* In the high-speed blender, combine all the ingredients and process until a thick purée forms. Thin with additional orange juice as needed to create a very smooth sauce.

**Assembly**—Place a tuile in the center of each plate. Place 2 teaspoons Honey Pastry Cream and 3 fig pieces over the tuile and sprinkle with a few pieces of the torn basil. Repeat the layering two more times and then top with a fourth tuile. Lightly brush the top tuile with honey. Spoon the Fig Sauce and the olive oil around the plate. Arrange any remaining fig pieces and torn basil leaves around the sauce.

**Wine Notes**—Figs, honey, brown spices—all these flavors demand a Chenin Blanc from the Loire Valley. Gaston Huet's Vouvrays are magical wines, and this dessert seems custom-made for them. His late-harvest 1989 Cuvée Constance smells of honeycombs and sweet spices. It is also full-bodied, but without the sticky sweetness that plagues many dessert wines.

## Serves 4

### Baklava Tuiles

$1/2$ cup golden flaxseed, soaked for 8 to 10 hours in 1 cup filtered water

$1/2$ cup maple sugar

$1/2$ small Fuji or Gala apple, peeled, cored, and chopped

$1/4$ cup golden flax meal

$1/2$ teaspoon freshly ground cinnamon

$3/4$ teaspoon vanilla extract

### Honey Pastry Cream

$1/2$ cup Star Thistle Gelato base, not frozen (see Appendices)

1 tablespoon chopped young Thai coconut meat

$1 1/2$ teaspoons raw cashews, soaked for 12 to 14 hours in filtered water and drained

$3/4$ teaspoon raw star thistle honey

$3/4$ teaspoon powdered agar-agar, dissolved in 2 tablespoons hot (118°F) filtered water

### Fig Sauce

1 cup chopped Black Mission figs

Juice of 1 orange, or as needed

2 tablespoons raw star thistle honey

12 Black Mission figs, stems trimmed and figs cut into eighths and tossed with 3 tablespoons raw star thistle honey

6 fresh basil leaves, torn into tiny pieces

Raw star thistle honey for brushing

4 teaspoons olive oil

# Michigan Sour Cherries with Vanilla Cream and Orange Sabayon

*It's hard to beat cherries and plums at the height of their season. Here, slightly tart Michigan cherries and meaty, not-too-sweet red plums are matched up with a satiny orange-scented sabayon and an opulent vanilla cream. The textures of the two sauces contrast sharply with the fruits, and at the same time provide an ideal level of sweetness that highlights their stunning flavors. Tarragon leaves deliver an exotic finish.*

**Method**—*To make the Orange Sabayon:* In a high-speed blender, combine the cashews, maple syrup, orange juice, orange pieces, coconut, vanilla extract, and maple sugar and process until smooth. Thin with more orange juice or maple syrup as needed to create a smooth, thick sauce.

*To make the Vanilla Cream:* In the high-speed blender, combine the coconut meat, cashews, dates, coconut water, and vanilla seeds and extract and process until smooth.

Pit 10 of the cherries, place them in the high-speed blender, and process until smooth. Pass the purée through a fine-mesh sieve. Halve and pit the remaining cherries. Using a sharp paring knife, cut each plum into circular slices 1/4 inch thick, cutting around the pit. Carefully lift off the slices.

**Assembly**—Spoon one-fourth of the Orange Sabayon in the center of each plate. Top with one-fourth of the Vanilla Cream. Arrange one-fourth each of the cherry halves and plum slices over the creams. Sprinkle with 1 teaspoon of the tarragon leaves, and drizzle the cherry juice around the plate.

**Wine Notes**—The cashews and maple syrup in the sabayon provide the dish with undertones and weight, while the sour cherries sing the high notes. Brachetto d'Acqui is a delicately sweet red wine made in Italy's Piedmont region. Its fresh berry fruitiness amplifies the flavor of the cherries, and its light sparkle refreshes the taste buds. Banfi's Rosa Regale, another good choice, is readily available and always a crowd pleaser.

## Serves 4

### Orange Sabayon

1/4 cup raw cashews, soaked for 10 to 12 hours in filtered water and drained

1 tablespoon maple syrup, or as needed

1 1/2 tablespoons freshly squeezed orange juice, or as needed

1/2 orange, peeled, seeds removed, and chopped

1/4 cup chopped young Thai coconut meat

1 1/2 teaspoons vanilla extract

2 teaspoons maple sugar

### Vanilla Cream

1 1/2 cups finely chopped young Thai coconut meat

1/4 cup raw cashews, soaked for 10 to 12 hours in filtered water and drained

7 dates, pitted

1/4 cup coconut water

1/4 teaspoon seeds from vanilla bean

1/4 teaspoon vanilla extract

30 Michigan sour cherries

4 small red plums

4 teaspoons fresh tiny tarragon leaves

# Trio of Gelatos

*The three gelatos can be served together or separately, and each is superbly accented with its own sauce. Furthermore, while each explodes with flavor and richness, each is also light and delicate. This is an ideal finale to a special meal.*

**Method**—*To make the Persimmon Gelato:* In a high-speed blender, combine all the ingredients and process until smooth. Freeze in an ice-cream maker according to the manufacturer's directions.

*To make the Pineapple Gelato:* In the high-speed blender, combine all the ingredients and process until smooth. Freeze in the ice-cream maker according to the manufacturer's directions.

*To make the Chocolate Gelato:* In the high-speed blender, combine all the ingredients and process until smooth. Freeze in the ice-cream maker according to the manufacturer's directions.

*To make the Passion Fruit Sauce:* Halve the passion fruits crosswise and scoop out the pulp and seeds.

*To make the Huckleberry Sauce:* In the high-speed blender, combine the huckleberries and lime juice and purée until smooth. Pass through a fine-mesh sieve.

*To make the Star Fruit Sauce:* In the high-speed blender, combine half of the star fruit wedges, the honey, and the lemon juice and process until smooth. Pour into a bowl, add the remaining star fruit wedges, and toss to coat.

**Assembly**—Place one-sixth of the Star Fruit Sauce at 12 o'clock on each plate and put a quenelle of the Pineapple Gelato over the sauce. Spoon one-sixth of the Huckleberry Sauce at 3 o'clock and put a quenelle of the Persimmon Gelato over the sauce. Spoon one-sixth of the Passion Fruit Sauce at 9 o'clock and spread it down to 6 o'clock, then place a quenelle of the Chocolate Gelato over the sauce.

**Wine Notes**—This collection of gelatos is exceptionally light and refreshing, and it needs a wine with similar characteristics. Muscat de Beaumes-de-Venise from Domaine de Durban is a lightly sweet dessert wine with the aroma of peaches and apricots. Although it is a fortified wine rather than a "raw" wine, such technicalities are quickly forgotten after tasting it with the gelatos.

## Serves 6

### Persimmon Gelato

2 tablespoons coconut milk

2 cups chopped persimmon

1/4 cup coconut water

2 tablespoons raw orange blossom honey

1/8 teaspoon freshly squeezed lime juice

Pinch of Celtic sea salt

### Pineapple Gelato

2 cups chopped pineapple

2 tablespoons coconut milk

2 tablespoons plus 1 teaspoon maple syrup

1/8 teaspoon freshly squeezed lime juice

Seeds from 1/4 vanilla bean (optional)

### Chocolate Gelato

1 1/2 cups Almond Milk (see Appendices)

1 cup coconut water

3/4 cup chopped young Thai coconut meat

1/4 cup date sugar

1/4 cup maple syrup

1/4 cup Green & Black's Organic cocoa powder

2 tablespoons coconut oil

Seeds from 1/4 vanilla bean

### Passion Fruit Sauce

2 passion fruits

### Huckleberry Sauce

1 cup huckleberries

1 tablespoon freshly squeezed lime juice

### Star Fruit Sauce

2 star fruits, cut into bite-sized wedges

2 tablespoons raw honey

2 teaspoons freshly squeezed lemon juice

# Black Mission Fig Tart
## with Walnut Cream

*The simplicity of the flavor structure cloaks the refined elegance of this dish, which has just the right balance of sweetness, richness, tartness, and creaminess. The recipe also lends itself to substituting other ingredients for the figs, such as peaches or Queen Ann cherries.*

**Method**—*To make the tart shells:* In a food processor, combine the Brazil nuts, walnuts, and figs and process until crumbly. Add the salt and process to combine. Divide the nut-fig mixture into 4 equal portions. On a nonstick drying sheet, form each portion into a 5-inch round, making the rounds as thin as possible. Using your fingers, form a slight indentation in each round to give the tart shell a shallow rim. Place the sheet on a dehydrator shelf and dehydrate at 105°F for 8 to 10 hours, or until the tart shells are just dry.

*To make the Walnut Cream:* Drain the walnuts and place on a dehydrator shelf. Dehydrate at 105°F for 4 hours, or until crisp. In a high-speed blender, combine the walnuts, maple syrup, and water and process until smooth. Set aside 8 tablespoons for the tart shells; reserve the remainder for another use.

*To prepare the figs:* Combine all the ingredients in a bowl and toss to mix.

*To make the Fruit Compote:* Just before serving, combine all the ingredients in a bowl and toss to mix.

**Assembly**—Place a tart shell in the center of each plate. Spoon 2 tablespoons of the Walnut Cream onto the tart shell in a smooth layer. Arrange 6 pieces of the figs in a pinwheel over the Walnut Cream. Spoon the Fruit Compote around the plate.

**Wine Notes**—The tart shell, made from Brazil nuts and walnuts, requires a wine with muscle. Philip Togni's Ca' Togni, made in minuscule amounts from old vines of the Black Hamburg grape, is a match for the richness of the tart shell. The wine is also an aromatic mix of jammy fruit and floral notes that enhances the pomegranate and huckleberries.

**Serves 4**

### Tart Shells

1 cup raw Brazil nuts, soaked for 8 to 10 hours in filtered water and drained

1 cup raw walnuts, soaked for 8 to 10 hours in filtered water and drained

1/2 cup dried Black Mission figs, chopped

Pinch of Celtic sea salt

### Walnut Cream

2 cups raw walnuts, soaked for 8 to 10 hours in filtered water

1/2 cup maple syrup

1/4 cup filtered water

### Figs

6 Black Mission figs, stems trimmed and each fig cut into 6 wedges

1 1/2 tablespoons raw lavender honey

1 teaspoon ground fresh lavender flowers (ground in a mortar)

### Fruit Compote

1/4 cup mandarin orange segments, supremed and cut into tiny wedges

3 tablespoons pomegranate seeds

3 tablespoons huckleberries

2 teaspoons fresh lemon verbena leaves, cut into very fine chiffonade

# Apple-Quince Pavé with Pecan-Maple Ice Cream

*One of the beauties of this simple-to-make preparation is that it can be served in almost any portion size. The satiny Pecan-Maple Ice Cream is the perfect accent to the layers of apple and quince that make up the pavé. Apple chips and pecans provide important textural notes, and a drizzle of Cinnamon Oil and wisps of lemon verbena add festive flavor notes. Pears would be a fine substitution for the apples.*

**Method**—*To make the pavé:* Line a 6-inch square pan with plastic wrap, allowing an overhang on 2 opposite sides. Combine the honey, lemon juice, and lemon zest in a small bowl and stir to mix. Brush the bottom of the lined pan with the lemon-honey mixture.

Cover the bottom of the lined pan with a layer of the Granny Smith apple slices, arranging them snugly. Brush the layer with some of the lemon-honey mixture. Top with a layer of the quince slices, brush it with more of the lemon-honey mixture, and then top with a layer of the Gala apple slices and again brush with the lemon-honey mixture. Repeat the layers until you have used all the fruit slices. Cover with the overhanging plastic wrap and press down gently with your hands. Top with another pan that fits inside the rim, then place a 2-pound weight on the second pan. Refrigerate for at least 1 hour or for up to 10 hours before serving.

When ready to serve, remove the weight and the second pan, then remove the pavé, using the plastic wrap to lift it out. Trim the edges with a sharp knife to create perfectly straight sides. Cut the pavé in half on the diagonal, and then cut each half into 4 triangles, for a total of 8 triangles.

*To make the Pecan-Maple Ice Cream:* Drain the pecans, reserving 1 cup of the water. In a high-speed blender, combine the pecans, the 1 cup water, and the maple syrup and process until smooth. Pass the purée through a fine-mesh sieve and freeze in an ice-cream maker according to the manufacturer's directions.

*To make the Sultana Sauce:* In the high-speed blender, combine all the ingredients and process until creamy. Pass the purée through a fine-mesh sieve.

*To make the Cinnamon Oil:* In the high-speed blender, combine all the ingredients and process for about 3 minutes, or until both cinnamons are incorporated. Tiny flecks of cinnamon will be visible. Transfer to a small container and let stand for 2 to 3 hours before using to allow the flavor to develop. Pass the oil through a fine-mesh sieve.

*To prepare the apple slices for garnish:* Arrange the apple slices on a dehydrator shelf, brush with the lemon juice, and dehydrate at 105°F for 3 to 4 hours, or until dry.

**Assembly**—Place a triangle of pavé in the center of each plate. Spoon one-eighth each of the Sultana Sauce and the Cinnamon Oil around the triangle. Sprinkle with 1 scant teaspoon of the lemon verbena and one-eighth of the pecans. Place a quenelle of the Pecan-Maple Ice Cream on the plate, and anchor an apple slice in the ice cream.

**Wine Notes**—The pavé offers tantalizing flavors of quince and apple that should not be overwhelmed by a syrupy, sticky sweet dessert wine. Quarts de Chaume from Domaine des Baumard puts a spotlight on those flavors, while continuing to support the bolder tastes of the Sultana Sauce and the ice cream.

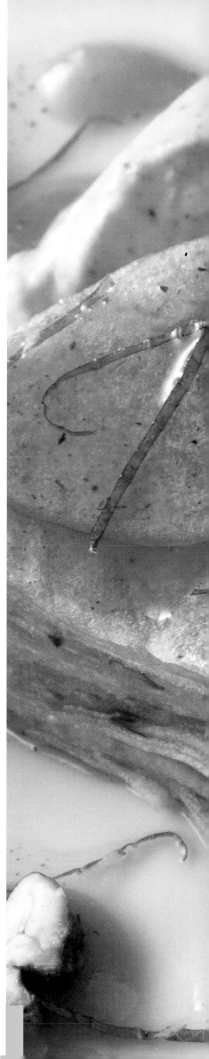

**Serves 8**

**Pavé**

$1/4$ cup raw orange blossom honey

1 tablespoon freshly squeezed
lemon juice

1 tablespoon grated lemon zest

1 Granny Smith apple, skin on,
halved, cored, and sliced
paper-thin lengthwise

1 quince, peeled, halved, cored,
and sliced paper-thin lengthwise

1 Gala apple, skin on,
halved, cored, and sliced
paper-thin lengthwise

**Pecan-Maple Ice Cream**

2 cups pecans, soaked for
8 to 10 hours in filtered water

$1/2$ cup maple syrup

**Sultana Sauce**

$1/2$ cup sultanas, soaked for 2 hours
in filtered water and drained

1 tablespoon freshly squeezed
lemon juice

1 tablespoon filtered water

**Cinnamon Oil**

$1/3$ cup grapeseed oil

2 teaspoons freshly
ground cinnamon

1 3-inch cinnamon stick, broken
into small pieces

**Garnish**

8 paper-thin Gala apple slices,
skin on, cut lengthwise from
whole apple

Freshly squeezed lemon juice
for brushing

2 tablespoons finely julienned
fresh lemon verbena leaves

8 pecan halves, sliced crosswise

APPLE-QUINCE PAVÉ WITH PECAN-MAPLE ICE CREAM

# Chocolate Cake Rolls with Chai Tea Gelato and Star Thistle Gelato

*These cake rolls are a stunning way to end a meal. The two gelatos haunt the palate with their refined complexity, while the accompanying sauces deepen the overall flavor, making their respective cake rolls all the more irresistible. Candied almonds, a nice textural counterpoint, are a crowning accent of richness.*

**Method**—*To make the Chocolate Cake:* Spread the almonds and sunflower seeds on a dehydrator shelf and dehydrate at 105°F for 6 hours, or until dry. In a food processor, combine the almonds, sunflower seeds, pine nuts, honey, cocoa powder, flax meal, apple, olive oil, shoyu, vanilla extract, and nutmeg and process while slowly adding the water. Continue to process until a smooth batter forms. Using an offset spatula, and using 2 cups batter for each sheet, spread the batter on 2 nonstick drying sheets, dividing it evenly and forming a 14-inch square on each sheet. Place the sheets on dehydrator shelves and dehydrate at 105°F for 5 hours. Flip the cakes onto the shelves and continue to dehydrate for 8 hours longer, or until dry but still pliable.

When the cakes are ready, using a sharp knife, trim the edges so that they are even, then cut each cake in half lengthwise. Each half will be about 13 1/2 inches long and 6 1/2 inches wide. Cover and chill.

*To make the Chai Tea Concentrate:* Combine all the ingredients in a bowl and whisk to combine thoroughly. Cover and refrigerate for at least 1 to 2 days or for up to 1 week to meld the flavors. Pour through a fine-mesh sieve into a clean container. Measure out 1/4 cup for making the Chai Tea Gelato and 1/4 cup for making the Chai Tea Sauce; cap the remainder tightly and refrigerate for another use. (You can add 1 to 2 tablespoons concentrate to nut milk made from 2 parts Almond Milk and 1 part Cashew Milk for a delicious drink.)

*To make the Chai Tea Gelato:* In a high-speed blender, combine all the ingredients and process until smooth. Freeze in an ice-cream maker according to the manufacturer's directions.

*To make the Chai Tea Sauce:* Combine the Almond Milk and Chai Tea Concentrate in a bowl and stir to mix.

*To make the Almond Milk Sauce:* In the high-speed blender, combine all the ingredients and process until smooth.

*To make the Candied Almonds:* Combine the almonds, maple sugar, and shoyu in a bowl and toss to coat the almonds evenly. Spread the almonds on a nonstick drying sheet on a dehydrator shelf and dehydrate at 105°F for 8 hours. Flip the almonds onto the dehydrator shelf and continue to dehydrate for about 16 hours longer, or until crisp. Chop coarsely and set aside.

Remove the cake strips from the refrigerator and place on a work surface. Divide the Chai Tea Gelato equally among 2 of the strips, spreading it evenly on top and covering two-thirds of the length of each strip. Starting at the covered end, roll up the cake strip like a jelly roll. Divide the Star Thistle Gelato equally among the remaining 2 cake strips, and spread and roll up in the same manner. Wrap each roll tightly in plastic wrap and place the rolls in the freezer for 1 hour before slicing for serving.

**Assembly**—Using a sharp, heavy knife, cut each cake roll into 4 equal pieces. Spoon a line of the Chai Tea Sauce and a line of the Almond Milk Sauce parallel to each other at an angle on each plate. Place 2 pieces of the Chai Tea Gelato–filled cake roll, cut side up, over the Chai Tea Sauce, and 2 pieces of the Star Thistle Gelato–filled cake roll, cut side up, over the Almond Milk Sauce. Sprinkle the Candied Almonds around the plate.

**Wine Notes**—Fausto Maculan makes some of greatest dessert wines in the world. His Acininobili, a blend of Vespaiola, Garganega, and Tocai grapes, competes with the finest Sauternes every year. This rich, full-bodied wine accentuates the nuttiness of the almonds in the chocolate cake rolls. The star thistle and chai tea remain vibrant flavors even with the unctuousness of the Maculan wine.

**Serves 4**

### Chocolate Cake

1 cup raw almonds, soaked for
12 hours in filtered water
and drained

$^1/_2$ cup raw sunflower seeds,
soaked for 6 hours in filtered
water and drained

1 cup raw pine nuts

$^1/_2$ cup raw honey

7 tablespoons Green & Black's
Organic cocoa powder

$^1/_4$ cup golden flax meal

$^1/_4$ cup finely diced,
peeled Fuji apple

2 tablespoons extra virgin olive oil

1 teaspoon nama shoyu

1 teaspoon vanilla extract

$^1/_4$ teaspoon freshly grated nutmeg

$^1/_4$ cup filtered water

### Chai Tea Concentrate

$^1/_2$ cup maple syrup

1 tablespoon plus $^3/_4$ teaspoon
ginger juice

1 $^1/_2$ teaspoons raw carob powder

1 teaspoon freshly
ground green cardamom

1 $^1/_2$ teaspoons freshly
ground cinnamon

$^1/_2$ teaspoon freshly
grated nutmeg

### Chai Tea Gelato

1 $^1/_2$ cups Cashew Milk
(see Appendices)

$^1/_2$ cup coconut water

$^3/_4$ cup chopped young Thai
coconut meat

6 tablespoons date sugar

$^1/_4$ cup Chai Tea Concentrate

3 tablespoons coconut oil

$^1/_4$ teaspoon seeds from
vanilla bean

### Chai Tea Sauce

$^3/_4$ cup Almond Milk
(see Appendices)

$^1/_4$ cup Chai Tea Concentrate

### Almond Milk Sauce

1 cup Almond Milk
(see Appendices)

$^1/_4$ cup chopped young Thai
coconut meat

1 tablespoon maple sugar

### Candied Almonds

$^1/_2$ cup le Plus Almonds, soaked
for 5 hours in filtered water,
drained, and patted dry

1 tablespoon maple sugar

$^1/_2$ teaspoon nama shoyu

3 cups Star Thistle Gelato
(see Appendices)

CHOCOLATE CAKE ROLLS WITH CHAI TEA GELATO
AND STAR THISTLE GELATO

# Banana Chocolate Tart with Caramel and Chocolate Sauces

*There may not be a better combination than bananas and chocolate, unless, of course, caramel and walnuts are added to the mix. This tart intoxicates through its remarkably sensual, intense flavor. It is the sort of dish that once you begin eating it, you are compelled to stop talking to others at the table. The child in every adult emerges when this tart is served!*

**Method**—*To make the tart shells:* Combine all the ingredients in a bowl and stir to mix well. Place 2 tablespoons of the mixture in the bottom of each of 4 ring molds each 2 inches in diameter. Pack the mixture firmly into the molds. (You will have more dough than you need for 4 molds. Because the tiny tart shells are fragile and time-consuming to make, it is a good idea to line additional ring molds with the remaining dough in case of breakage.) Place the molds on a nonstick drying sheet on a dehydrator shelf and dehydrate at 105°F for 3 hours. Remove the tart shells from the drying sheet and dehydrate directly on the shelf for about 10 hours longer, or until just dry.

*To make the Caramel Sauce:* Drain the cashews, pat them dry, and then measure them. You should have $1/4$ cup; discard any excess. In a high-speed blender, combine the cashews, Cashew Milk, honey, Date Paste, and maple syrup and process until smooth. Strain the purée through a fine-mesh sieve. Set aside 4 tablespoons for the tarts; reserve the remainder for another use.

**Assembly**—Spoon 1 tablespoon of the Mexican Chocolate Sauce in a circle on each plate. Put a tart shell on top of the sauce. Spread 2 tablespoons of the Chocolate Fudge–Almond on the tart shell. Arrange 7 banana slices on top. Drizzle 1 tablespoon Caramel Sauce over the bananas and on the plate. Sprinkle with the Honey Walnuts.

**Wine Notes**—This rich tart requires a wine with serious heft and sweetness because of the golden rule that says, "The wine must always be sweeter than the dessert." Trevor Jones's Old Tokay from Australia's Barossa Valley, although not a "raw" wine because a spirit has been added, makes for too perfect a combination to be shunted aside. Its concentrated chocolate and caramel flavors are truly unbelievable with the syrupy richness of the sauces.

**Serves 4**

**Tart Shells**

$3/4$ cup plus 2 tablespoons sprouted flour

1 tablespoon maple syrup

2 tablespoons plus 1 teaspoon extra virgin olive oil

Seeds from $1/2$ vanilla bean

Pinch of Celtic sea salt

**Caramel Sauce**

3 heaping tablespoons raw cashews, soaked for 8 hours in filtered water

$1/4$ cup plus 1 teaspoon Cashew Milk (see Appendices)

2 tablespoons raw dark honey

2 tablespoons Date Paste (see Appendices)

2 tablespoons maple syrup

4 tablespoons Mexican Chocolate Sauce (see Appendices)

8 tablespoons Chocolate Fudge–Almond (see Appendices)

28 banana slices

4 tablespoons Honey Walnuts (see Appendices), broken

# Chocolate Chip Cookies and
# Chocolate Truffles

*These cookies and truffles are fanciful and fun, but at the same time are very serious preparations. They can be eaten as snacks or offered as the exquisite finale for a special dinner. The truffles in particular burst with flavor, and it is almost impossible not to devour the warm cookies right out of the dehydrator!*

**Method**—*To make the chocolate truffle base and chocolate chips:* In a food processor, combine all the ingredients and process until smooth and thick. Measure out 1 1/2 cups, cover, and refrigerate; bring to room temperature before making the truffles. To make the chocolate chips, spoon the balance of the mixture into a pastry bag fitted with a very small plain tip, and pipe chips 1/4 inch in diameter onto nonstick drying sheets, forming 200 chips in all. Place the sheets on dehydrator shelves and dehydrate the chips at 105°F for 8 hours. Remove the chips from the drying sheets and dehydrate them directly on the shelves for 12 hours longer, or until dry and firm.

*To make the Chocolate Chip Cookies:* In a stand mixer fitted with the paddle attachment, combine the sprouted flour, coconut butter, maple syrup, vanilla seeds, and salt. Beat on medium speed until the mixture comes together. Stir in the chocolate chips and Honey Walnuts. Using your hands, shape the dough into rounds 2 to 3 inches in diameter and 1/4 to 1/2 inch thick and place on nonstick drying sheets. Place the sheets on dehydrator shelves and dehydrate the cookies at 105°F for 6 hours, or until firm. Remove the cookies from the drying sheets and dehydrate them directly on the shelves for 8 to 10 hours longer, or until they have the desired crispness. The cookies should be hard yet still moist. Set aside 8 cookies for the dish. Store the remainder in an airtight container at room temperature for up to 3 days.

*To make the Tahini Orange Truffles:* In the food processor, combine the tahini, honey, and orange zest and process until well mixed. Using your palms, shape the tahini mixture into small balls about 1/2 inch in diameter. Scoop up a little of the truffle base—it will have the consistency of a soft fudge—and form it around the filling, first using your fingers to form a thin, even layer and then rolling the truffle between your palms to smooth the round. Roll in five-spice powder to coat lightly. Count out 4 truffles for the dish and refrigerate for 1 hour. Store the remainder in the refrigerator for up to 2 weeks.

*To make the Curried Truffles:* In the food processor, combine the walnuts, honey, and cinnamon and process until well mixed. Using your palms, shape the walnut mixture into small balls about 1/2 inch in diameter. Scoop up a little of the truffle base—it will have the consistency of a soft fudge—and form it around the filling, first using your fingers to form a thin, even layer and then rolling the truffle between your palms to smooth the round. Roll in the spice mix to coat lightly. Count out 4 truffles for the dish and refrigerate for 1 hour. Store the remainder in the refrigerator for up to 2 weeks.

*To make the Lemon Truffles:* In the food processor, combine the sprouted flour, sprouted meal, coconut butter, maple syrup, and salt and process until well mixed. Using your palms, shape the mixture into small balls about 1/2 inch in diameter. Scoop up a little of the truffle base—it will have the consistency of a soft fudge—and form it around the filling, first using your fingers to form a thin, even layer and then rolling the truffle between your palms to smooth the round shape. Roll in the lemon zest to coat lightly. Count out 4 truffles for the dish and refrigerate for 1 hour. Store the remainder in the refrigerator for up to 2 weeks.

**Assembly**—Cut 1 truffle of each type in half and place on each plate. Arrange 2 cookies and 4 gooseberries near the truffles. Sprinkle the plate with the honey granules.

**Wine Notes**—One of the first pairings that every child learns is milk and cookies. There is nothing that quite compares with a glass of cold milk alongside a plate of freshly baked cookies. As nice as it would be to mate a sweet wine with this course, none could match the suitability of a tall glass of Almond Milk (see Appendices).

Serves 4

### Chocolate Truffle Base and Chocolate Chips

1 cup raw cashew butter

1 cup maple syrup

1 cup Green & Black's Organic cocoa powder or raw carob powder

1/4 teaspoon seeds from vanilla bean

1 tablepoon nama shoyu

### Chocolate Chip Cookies

1 3/4 cups sprouted flour

6 tablespoons coconut butter

2 tablespoons maple syrup

Seeds from 1/2 vanilla bean

Pinch of Celtic sea salt

200 chocolate chips (about 8 ounces)

1/2 cup Honey Walnuts
(see Appendices), broken

### Tahini Orange Truffles

1/4 cup raw tahini

3 tablespoons raw clover honey

1 tablespoon grated orange zest

1/2 cup chocolate truffle base

Five-spice powder for dusting

### Curried Truffles

1 cup raw walnuts, chopped

1/2 cup raw clover honey

1 1/2 teaspoons freshly ground cinnamon

1/2 cup chocolate truffle base

Indian Spice Mix (see Appendices) for dusting

### Lemon Truffles

3/4 cup sprouted flour

1/2 cup sprouted meal

2 tablespoons coconut butter

2 tablespoons maple syrup

Pinch of Celtic sea salt

1/2 cup chocolate truffle base

Lemon zest shaved with a Microplane grater for dusting

16 tiny golden gooseberries, husks twisted at top

2 tablespoons honey granules

CHOCOLATE CHIP COOKIES AND CHOCOLATE TRUFFLES

# BEVERAGES

*Healthful and refreshing beverages are wonderful additions to any sound lifestyle. They take just moments to prepare, are surprisingly good thirst quenchers, and can quickly cure any midday snack cravings. Use these recipes as guidelines only, changing them according to what fruits and vegetables are in season or what you might be craving at the moment. For optimal flavor and nutrition, always consume the beverages as soon as possible after making them.*

## Red Roxie

Put the apples, beets, and ginger through a heavy-duty juicer, then stir in the lemon juice.

**Serves 2**

4 Fuji or Gala apples, skin on, cored and cut into eights

2 small red beets, peeled and chopped

$1/2$-inch piece fresh ginger

3 tablespoons freshly squeezed lemon or lime juice

## Green Roxie

Put all the ingredients through a heavy-duty juicer.

**Serves 2**

5 dino kale leaves with stems intact

5 dandelion leaves with stems intact

5 celery stalks, chopped

3 Fuji or Gala apples, skin on, cored and cut into eights

$1/2$-inch piece fresh ginger

1 cup chopped, peeled red beets

2 cups strawberries, hulled

1 small Fuji apple, skin on, cored
and cut into eighths

1 tablespoon freshly squeezed
lime juice

## Red Beet, Strawberry, and Apple

Put the beets, strawberries, and apple through a heavy-duty juicer,
then stir in the lime juice.

2 cups chopped pineapple

2 celery stalks, chopped

1 $^1/_2$ teaspoons fresh
rosemary leaves

$^1/_2$ cup freshly squeezed
orange juice

## Pineapple, Orange, Rosemary, and Celery

Put the pineapple, celery, and rosemary through a heavy-duty juicer,
then stir in the orange juice.

1 cup coconut water

$^1/_4$ cup chopped young Thai
coconut meat

2 tablespoons chopped
fresh lemongrass

2 cups chopped pineapple

## Coconut, Lemongrass, and Pineapple

Combine all the ingredients in a high-speed blender and process
until smooth.

## Blackberry, Prickly Pear, Asian Pear, and Orange with Thai Lime Leaf

Put the prickly pear, blackberries, Asian pear, and lime leaf through a heavy-duty juicer, then stir in the orange juice. If necessary, strain through a fine-mesh sieve before serving.

Serves 2

1 cup chopped, peeled
prickly pear

1 cup blackberries

1 cup chopped, peeled Asian pear

1 fresh Thai lime leaf, chopped

1 cup freshly squeezed
orange juice

## Cucumber, Mint, Apple, Celery, and Key Lime

Put the cucumbers, apple, celery, and spearmint leaves through a heavy-duty juicer. Strain through a medium-mesh sieve into glasses. Drizzle 1 teaspoon lime juice over the top of each serving.

Serves 2

2 cucumbers, peeled and
halved lengthwise

2 cups chopped, peeled Granny
Smith apple

2 celery stalks, chopped

8 fresh spearmint leaves

2 teaspoons freshly squeezed
Key lime juice

## Fennel, Grapefruit, Celery, and Apple

Put the fennel, celery, and apple through a heavy-duty juicer, then stir in the grapefruit juice. Strain through a fine-mesh sieve into glasses.

Serves 2

3 cups chopped fennel

2 celery stalks, chopped

1 Braeburn apple, skin on, cored
and cut into eighths

1 cup freshly squeezed
grapefruit juice

**Serves 2**

2 cups cranberries

1 cup chopped pineapple

1 cup chopped young Thai
coconut meat

1 cup coconut water

$1/4$ teaspoon seeds from vanilla bean

$1/4$ cup freshly squeezed orange juice

1 tablespoon maple sugar

$1/4$ teaspoon freshly
ground cinnamon

**Serves 2**

1 mango, peeled, pitted,
and chopped

1 blood orange, peeled

$1/2$ yellow papaya, peeled, seeded,
and chopped

1 tablespoon maple sugar

$1/2$ cup coconut water

1 tablespoon fresh spearmint
leaves, chopped

$1/2$ cup freshly squeezed orange juice

$1 1/2$ cups crushed ice

1 passion fruit, halved and pulp
and seeds scooped out

## Cranberry, Vanilla, and Cinnamon

Combine all the ingredients in a high-speed blender and process
until smooth.

## Mango, Blood Orange, and Spearmint

Combine all the ingredients except the passion fruit in a high-speed
blender and process until smooth. Pour into chilled glasses and spoon
the passion fruit pulp and seeds on top, dividing them evenly.

## Blueberry, Apple, and Vanilla

Combine all the ingredients in a high-speed blender and process until smooth.

**Serves 2**

1 1/2 cups blueberries

1/2 cup chopped banana

1/2 cup freshly squeezed orange juice

1/4 cup maple syrup

1/4 teaspoon seeds from vanilla bean

1 Braeburn apple, skin on, cored and chopped

2 teaspoons freshly squeezed lime juice

1 1/4 cups crushed ice

## Mango, Coconut, and Curry

Combine the coconut meat and coconut water in a high-speed blender and process until smooth. Remove half of the purée from the blender and reserve. Add the remaining ingredients to the coconut purée in the blender and process until smooth. Pour into chilled glasses and spoon an equal amount of the reserved coconut mixture on top of each glass. Sprinkle each serving with a pinch of spice mix.

**Serves 2**

1/4 cup chopped young Thai coconut meat

1/2 cup coconut water

1 mango, peeled, pitted, and chopped

1/4 cup raw cashews, soaked for 8 hours in filtered water and drained

1/4 cup Cashew Milk (see Appendices)

1 tablespoon freshly squeezed Key lime juice

1/4 cup freshly squeezed orange juice

1/4 cup maple sugar

1 1/2 cups crushed ice

1 teaspoon Indian Spice Mix (see Appendices) or sweet curry powder, plus extra for garnish

## Huckleberry, Orange, and Maple

Serves 2

1 1/2 cups huckleberries

1/2 banana, peeled and chopped

1 cup freshly squeezed orange juice

2 tablespoons maple sugar

2 tablespoons maple syrup

1/2 cup raw cashews, soaked for
8 hours in filtered water and drained

1 cup Cashew Milk (see Appendices)

2 whole cloves

2 cups crushed ice

Combine all the ingredients in a high-speed blender and process until smooth.

## Pink Guava and Hibiscus

Serves 2

2 cups chopped, peeled very ripe
pink guava

1/2 cup chopped mango

1/2 cup Cashew Milk (see Appendices)

3 tablespoons maple sugar

3/4 cup freshly squeezed orange juice

2 tablespoons dried hibiscus leaves,
steeped in 1/2 cup filtered water
for 1 hour

Combine all the ingredients in a high-speed blender and process until smooth.

## Prickly Pear and Pomegranate

Serves 2

1 1/2 cups chopped, peeled
prickly pear

Seeds from 1 pomegranate

3/4 cup freshly squeezed orange juice

1/4 cup Cashew Milk (see Appendices)

1/4 cup chopped banana

1 1/2 teaspoons minced, peeled
fresh ginger

2 cups crushed ice

Combine all the ingredients in a high-speed blender and process until smooth.

## French Melon, Celery, and Mint

Put the melon, apple, and celery through a heavy-duty juicer and pour into a pitcher. Stir in the Cashew Milk, maple sugar, lime juice, and orange juice. Crush the mint leaves with the ice, add to the pitcher, and stir to mix.

Serves 2

1 1/2 cups chopped French melon

1/4 cup chopped, peeled Granny Smith apple

2 celery stalks, chopped

1/4 cup Cashew Milk (see Appendices)

2 tablespoons maple sugar

Juice of 3 limes

1/4 cup freshly squeezed orange juice

12 fresh mint leaves

1 1/2 cups crushed ice

## Bing Cherry, Lemongrass, and Hibiscus

Combine 2 cups of the cherries, the hibiscus water, Cashew Milk, lemongrass, and 1 tablespoon of the maple sugar in a high-speed blender and process until smooth. Strain through a fine-mesh sieve and return to the blender. Add the remaining 1 cup cherries and 1 tablespoon maple sugar and the ice and process until smooth.

Serves 2

3 cups Bing cherries, pitted

3 tablespoons dried hibiscus leaves, steeped in 1 1/4 cups filtered water for 1 hour, strained, leaves discarded, and water reserved

1/4 cup Cashew Milk (see Appendices)

1/2 cup chopped fresh lemongrass

2 tablespoons maple sugar

1 1/2 cups crushed ice

## Cucumber-Lime Water

Combine the chopped cucumbers, mint, water, and lime juice in a high-speed blender and process until smooth. Strain through a fine-mesh sieve into a pitcher. Add the salt, maple sugar, and ice and stir to mix. Pour into chilled glasses and garnish with the cucumber slices.

Serves 2

2 English cucumbers, peeled and chopped

8 fresh mint leaves

1 cup bottled water

Juice of 3 limes

Pinch of Celtic sea salt

2 tablespoons maple sugar

2 cups crushed ice

4 thin cucumber slices

APPENDICES

# Equipment

*The equipment used in the preparation of raw cuisine is for the most part commonplace, rather than exotic, and you probably already own some, if not all, of it. In addition to the seven items described here, you will need everyday tools, such as good knives and cutting boards, variously sized whisks, offset and other spatulas, an assortment of sieves, a variety of mixing bowls and spoons, a selection of ring molds and terrines, and an instant-read thermometer for testing the temperature of liquids.*

## Dehydrator

Most dehydrators designed for home use are small, lightweight counter-top units, and there are a number of reputable brands on the market. I have an Excalibur dehydrator at my house, and I have found that it is easier to use than many other brands for two reasons: the trays are front loaded—like an oven—rather than top loaded, and it has an adjustable thermostat. Excalibur dehydrators come in three sizes: a 4-tray model with 4 square feet of drying space and a 4-inch fan with a 220-watt motor; a 5-tray model with 8 square feet of drying space and a 5-inch fan with a 400-watt motor; and a 9-tray model with 15 square feet of drying space and a 7-inch fan with a 600-watt motor. Excalibur also sells nonstick drying sheets for use in their units. The dehydrators range in price from about $130 to almost twice that amount.

## Food Processor

Most food processors on the market are great, and if you already have one at home, it is most likely sufficient for preparing raw cuisine. If it is an older piece of equipment or if you use it a lot, however, you should check the blade for sharpness. Take a dull blade to a professional knife sharpener, or contact the manufacturer or a local knife store about purchasing a new blade.

Our recipes were tested in an 11-cup food processor. If yours is smaller, simply process the mixture in two batches.

## Heavy-Duty Juicer

I use the Champion brand juicer, which is both a masticating juicer and, with a blank plate in place, a homogenizer. It is ideal for making not only juices of all kinds, but also for turning out butters, ice creams, and nut cheeses. The company, which has been in business for over half a century, makes a home model and a heavy-duty industrial model. I recommend the latter, which retails for about $230.

## High-Speed Blender

At the restaurant, I use two commercial high-speed blenders, the Vita-Mix and the K-Tec Blendtec. Each is outfitted with a 4-quart beaker and has variable-speed control. Both also have a comparable home model. The Vita-Mix home version is the TurboBlend 4500, which has a 2-horsepower, 2-speed motor and comes with a 5-year warranty. It retails for about $400. The Blendtec home model, the Champ HP3, has a 3-horsepower, 10-speed motor and an 8-year warranty. It retails for about the same price as the Vita-Mix.

These high-speed blenders, which break down even the toughest fibers in fruits and vegetables, are incomparable for making creamy dressings, soups, sorbets, ice creams, and more. However, if you have a blender at home that you are happy with and don't want to invest in a high-speed unit, you can use what you have. When making some recipes, you may not get as smooth or creamy a product as you would with a high-speed blender, and you may need to strain the purée through a fine-mesh sieve to eliminate any fibers or other coarse bits.

## Ice-Cream Maker

At the restaurant, I use the Swiss-made Pacojet ice-cream maker, a high-powered countertop commercial unit—about the size of a single-port espresso machine—that weighs only about 30 pounds and plugs into a regular 110-watt outlet. It processes frozen mixtures at a rapid rate (2,000 rpm), creating wonderfully smooth and creamy ice creams and sorbets. Because the Pacojet produces such a superb texture in the finished product, I find that I can use less sweetener in the base recipe.

The Pacojet is available for home use, but is quite costly at about $2,500. However, a regular home ice-cream maker will work just fine. You can also use the Champion or similar heavy-duty juicer if you freeze the ice-cream base in ice-cube trays and then homogenize it in the juicer.

## Spice Grinder

I use a variety of spice grinders, from an old-fashioned mortar and pestle that my parents carried home from a trip to Bali to an electric-powered Sumeet grinder, manufactured by a company based in Canada. The Sumeet is the high-quality replacement for the coffee grinder commonly used for grinding spices at home. It has a $1/2$-horsepower, 400-watt motor that quickly transforms the toughest seeds and grains into a fine powder and is powerful enough to make pastes. It is also easier to clean than a coffee grinder. The Sumeet retails for under $100. You can buy heavy-duty stone mortars and pestles at local Asian food stores.

## Stand Mixer

A good-quality, heavy-duty stand mixer is ideal for combining some mixtures, especially dessert batters and doughs. It should have a paddle attachment and a good, solid motor. If you already have only a handheld mixer, it can be used instead on all but the stiffest doughs.

—RK

# Basic Recipes

## Almond Milk and Almond Flour

*To make the milk:* In a high-speed blender, combine the almonds and water and blend until creamy. Line a large sieve with a double thickness of cheesecloth and place over a bowl. Pour the almond mixture into the sieve and let drain, then grab the corners of the cheesecloth, hold together securely, and squeeze the cheesecloth to extract all of the milk. Reserve the pulp in the sieve for making the flour. Transfer the milk to a covered container and refrigerate for up to 3 days.

*To make the flour:* Using an offset spatula, spread the pulp on a nonstick drying sheet on a dehydrator shelf. Dehydrate at 105°F for 24 hours, or until completely dry. Transfer the dehydrated pulp to a food processor and grind to a silky flour. Store in an airtight container in the refrigerator for up to 3 days.

Yield: 4 1/2 cups milk; 2 1/2 to 3 cups flour

3 cups raw almonds, soaked for 10 to 12 hours in filtered water, rinsed, and drained

6 cups filtered water

## Basil Oil

To make an oil with the brightest green result, blanch the basil, spinach, and parsley in boiling salted water for 45 seconds, then drain, immediately shock in ice water (this sets the color), and drain again. Squeeze to extract any excess water, then chop the greens coarsely. If you are adhering to a strict raw diet, omit this step and simply chop the raw greens coarsely. In a high-speed blender, combine the chopped greens and olive and canola oils and process for 3 to 4 minutes, or until the mixture is bright green. Pour into a container with a tight-fitting lid, cover, and refrigerate for 1 day.

The next day, strain the oil through a fine-mesh sieve and discard the solids. Return to the container and refrigerate for 1 day, then decant and use immediately or refrigerate for up to 1 week.

Yield: 3/4 cup

1/2 cup firmly packed fresh basil leaves

1/2 cup firmly packed spinach leaves

1/4 cup firmly packed fresh flat-leaf parsley leaves

1/4 cup extra virgin olive oil

1 cup grapeseed oil

## Cashew Cheese

In a high-speed blender or a Champion juicer with the blank plate in place, process the cashews until smooth. Transfer to a bowl and stir in the Rejuvelac and salt, mixing well. Line a sieve with a double thickness of cheesecloth and place over a bowl. Transfer the mixture to the sieve, drape the cheesecloth over the top, and leave in a warm place to ripen for 12 hours.

Remove the cheese from the cloth-lined sieve. Shape the mixture into a round, place in a covered container, and refrigerate for at least 24 hours, or until it firms up. Use immediately, or store in an airtight container in the refrigerator for up to 3 days.

The cheese can also be purchased directly from Roxanne's restaurant; call 415.924.5004 or visit www.roxraw.com.

Yield: 3 cups

3 cups raw cashews, soaked for 10 to 12 hours in filtered water and drained

1/4 cup Rejuvelac (page 195)

1/2 teaspoon Celtic sea salt

## Cashew Milk

To make Cashew Milk, follow the directions for Almond Milk, substituting 3 cups raw cashews for the almonds.

## Chocolate Fudge–Almond

**Yield: 2 cups**

1 cup raw almond butter, at room temperature

$^1/_2$ cup maple syrup

$^1/_2$ cup Green & Black's Organic cocoa powder

Seeds from $^1/_4$ vanilla bean

1 $^1/_2$ teaspoons nama shoyu

In a food processor, combine all the ingredients and process until smooth. The mixture will have the consistency of ganache. Use immediately, or store in a covered container in the refrigerator for up to 2 weeks.

## Chocolate Sauce

**Yield: 1 $^1/_2$ cups**

1 cup Chocolate Fudge–Almond (see above)

$^1/_4$ cup filtered water

2 tablespoons plus 1 teaspoon maple syrup

Combine all the ingredients in a bowl and whisk together vigorously. Use immediately, or store in a covered container in the refrigerator for up to 2 weeks.

## Curry Oil

In a high-speed blender, combine all the ingredients and process for 2 to 3 minutes, or until the outside of the blender container is warm. Pour into a glass jar or bowl, cover, and let stand overnight. The next day, strain through a coffee filter (do not press on the contents of the filter) into a container with a tight-fitting lid. Use immediately, or store in the refrigerator for up to 2 weeks.

**Yield: 1 cup**

2 tablespoons Indian Spice Mix (page 194)

1 clove garlic

$1/2$ teaspoon freshly ground turmeric

$1/8$ teaspoon freshly ground cayenne pepper

6 grains smoked salt

$1/4$ teaspoon Celtic sea salt

1 cup olive oil

## Date Paste

In a food processor, combine the dates and water and process until completely smooth. Use immediately, or store in a covered container in the refrigerator for up to 2 weeks.

**Yield: 1 rounded cup**

1 cup pitted Barhi dates

$1/2$ cup filtered water

## Dragon Crackers

Combine the flaxseed and water in a bowl and soak for 6 to 8 hours, or until the seeds absorb all of the water. In a food processor, combine the soaked seeds, shoyu, maple sugar, chili powder, garam masala, cayenne, onion, and garlic and process until smooth. Using an offset spatula, spread the flaxseed mixture in a $1/8$-inch-thick layer on nonstick drying sheets. Place on dehydrator shelves and dehydrate at 105°F for 4 hours, or until firm enough to flip the cracker sheets onto the dehydrator shelves. Once the sheets are on the shelves, cut into $1/2$ by 3-inch pieces, and continue to dehydrate for about 24 hours longer, or until crisp. Use immediately, or store in an airtight container at room temperature for up to 2 weeks.

To make cracker crumbs, place the crackers in a heavy-duty plastic bag and crush with a rolling pin.

The crackers can also be purchased directly from Roxanne's restaurant; call 415.924.5004 or visit www.roxraw.com.

**Yield: About 30 crackers**

1 $1/2$ cups golden flaxseed

2 $1/2$ cups filtered water

2 tablespoons nama shoyu

2 tablespoons maple sugar

1 $1/2$ teaspoons chili powder

$1/2$ teaspoon garam masala

$1/2$ teaspoon freshly ground cayenne pepper

$1/2$ teaspoon minced onion

$1/2$ teaspoon minced garlic

Yield: 1 ¹/₄ cups

1 cup Cashew Cheese (page 190)

4 teaspoons filtered water

1 teaspoon minced shallot

¹/₄ teaspoon freshly squeezed
lemon juice

¹/₂ teaspoon large flake
nutritional yeast

¹/₄ teaspoon Celtic sea salt,
or to taste

1 teaspoon chopped fresh basil

1 teaspoon chopped fresh thyme

Yield: ¹/₂ cup

¹/₄ cup firmly packed chopped
fresh chives

¹/₄ cup firmly packed fresh
flat-leaf parsley leaves

¹/₄ cup firmly packed
watercress leaves

¹/₂ cup grapeseed oil

¹/₄ cup extra virgin olive oil

Yield: 3 cups

3 cups raw walnuts, soaked for
6 to 8 hours in filtered water,
drained, and patted dry

6 tablespoons honey granules

¹/₄ teaspoon Celtic sea salt

¹/₄ teaspoon freshly
ground cinnamon

## Herb Cheese

Combine the Cashew Cheese, water, shallot, lemon juice, yeast,
and ¹/₄ teaspoon salt in a bowl and stir until thoroughly mixed. Stir
in the basil and thyme until evenly distributed. Taste and adjust with
additional salt, if needed. Use immediately, or store in a covered
container in the refrigerator for up to 3 days.

## Herb Oil

To make an oil with the brightest green result, in a small sauté pan,
sauté the chives, parsley, and watercress over medium heat in 1 tablespoon of the grapeseed oil for 2 minutes, or until wilted. Immediately
shock in ice water (this sets the color) and drain, squeezing to extract
any excess water, then chop coarsely. If you are adhering to a strict
raw diet, omit this step and simply chop the raw greens coarsely.
In a high-speed blender, combine the chopped greens, the remaining
7 tablespoons grapeseed oil or the ¹/₂ cup oil if you have not sautéed
the herbs, and the olive oil and process for 3 to 4 minutes, or until the
mixture is bright green. Pour into a container with a tight-fitting lid,
cover, and refrigerate for 1 day.

The next day, strain the oil through a fine-mesh sieve and discard the
solids. Return to the container and refrigerate for 1 day, then decant
and use immediately or refrigerate for up to 2 weeks.

## Honey Walnuts

Combine the walnuts, honey granules, salt, and cinnamon in a bowl
and toss to coat the nuts evenly with the other ingredients. Spread
the nuts on a nonstick drying sheet on a dehydrator shelf and dehydrate
at 105°F for 12 hours. Transfer the nuts to the shelf, spreading them
evenly, and continue to dehydrate for 24 hours longer, or until crisp.
Use immediately, or store in an airtight container at room temperature
for up to 1 week.

## Indian Spice Mix

Stir together all the ingredients in a small bowl until well mixed. Transfer to a jar, cover tightly, and store at room temperature for up to 1 month.

**Yield:** 1/2 cup

2 tablespoons freshly ground cinnamon

2 tablespoons freshly ground green cardamom

2 tablespoons freshly ground coriander

2 tablespoons freshly ground cumin

## Mexican Chocolate Sauce

Proceed as directed for the Chocolate Sauce, whisking in 1/2 teaspoon freshly ground cinnamon with the other ingredients.

## Pickled Garlic and Garlic Chips

*To make the Pickled Garlic:* Combine the cider vinegar, wine vinegar, water, peppercorns, salt, and chiles in a bowl and whisk until well mixed. Place the garlic cloves in a glass jar with a tight-fitting lid and pour in the vinegar mixture; it should immerse the garlic cloves completely. Tuck the bay leaves and oregano sprig in among the garlic cloves. Cap tightly and refrigerate for 1 week before using. The garlic will keep in the refrigerator for up to 1 month.

*To make the Garlic Chips:* Remove the pickled cloves from the brine and slice very thinly lengthwise. Arrange the slices on a dehydrator shelf and dehydrate at 105°F for 12 to 14 hours, or until dry. Use immediately, or store in an airtight container at room temperature for up to 1 week.

**Yield: 1 cup whole cloves; 1/2 cup chips**

2 cups apple cider vinegar

1/2 cup white wine vinegar

1 cup filtered water

1 1/2 tablespoons mixed peppercorns

1 1/2 teaspoons Celtic sea salt

1 teaspoon Thai chiles

1 cup garlic cloves, peeled but left whole

2 bay leaves

1 oregano sprig

$1/2$ cup raw pine nuts, soaked for
6 hours in filtered water and drained

$1/4$ cup filtered water

2 tablespoons extra virgin olive oil

$1 1/2$ tablespoons freshly squeezed
lemon juice

Celtic sea salt

2 cups raw pine nuts, soaked for
6 hours in filtered water and drained

$1 1/2$ cups Rejuvelac (below)

1 tablespoon Celtic sea salt

$1 1/2$ tablespoons large flake
nutritional yeast

$1/2$ cup wheat or rye berries

Filtered water as needed

## Pine Nut Mayonnaise

In a high-speed blender, combine the pine nuts, water, olive oil, lemon juice, and onion powder and process until a mayonnaiselike consistency forms. Season to taste with salt. The mixture will thicken as it sits; thin as needed with filtered water. Use immediately, or store in a covered container in the refrigerator for up to 5 days.

## Rawmesan

In a high-speed blender, combine the pine nuts and Rejuvelac and process until the mixture is thick and creamy. Pour into a small bowl, cover with a kitchen towel, and let stand in a warm place for 12 to 14 hours, or until the mixture smells like it has begun to ferment. It will have a yeasty odor.

Stir in the salt and yeast, mixing carefully. Using an offset spatula, spread the pine nut mixture in a $1/8$-inch-thick layer on nonstick drying sheets. Place on dehydrator shelves and dehydrate at 105°F for 10 to 14 hours, or until it breaks easily into dime-sized flakes. Use immediately, or transfer to a covered container and store in the refrigerator for up to several weeks.

## Rejuvelac

In the evening, place the wheat or rye berries in a sprouting jar, and fill the jar with water. Let stand overnight. The next morning, drain the berries and spread them on a sprouting rack (a plastic or glass rectangular container lined with wet paper towels can be substituted). Leave them to sprout for 1 to 2 days, rinsing them 3 times a day. They are ready when $1/4$-inch tails have emerged.

Place the sprouts in a wide container with at least 3-inch-high sides and add 4 cups filtered water. Let stand in a warm spot for 12 to 14 hours, or until the liquid smells slightly fermented.

Strain off the liquid (this is the Rejuvelac) into a clean jar. Use immediately, or cover tightly and store in the refrigerator for up to 5 days. The same sprouts may be used 3 more times to make additional Rejuvelac. (See glossary for information on commercial Rejuvelac.)

## Sour Cream

In a high-speed blender, combine the coconut meat, cashews, olive oil, lemon juice, Date Paste, and salt and process until smooth. Transfer to a bowl and stir in water as needed to thin to the consistency of sour cream. Use immediately, or store in a covered container in the refrigerator for up to 1 week.

**Yield: About 2 cups**

3/4 cup chopped young Thai coconut meat

1/3 cup raw cashews, soaked for 10 to 12 hours in filtered water and drained

3 tablespoons extra virgin olive oil

2 tablespoons freshly squeezed lemon juice

1 teaspoon Date Paste (page 192)

1/2 teaspoon Celtic sea salt

About 1/2 cup filtered water

## Spicy Cashews

Place the cashews in a bowl and add the maple sugar, chili powder, salt, and cayenne. Toss to coat. Spread the cashews on a nonstick drying sheet on a dehydrator shelf and dehydrate at 105°F for 24 hours, or until crisp.

**Yield: About 1 cup**

1 cup raw cashews, soaked for 10 to 12 hours in filtered water, drained, and patted dry

1 tablespoon maple sugar

1 1/2 teaspoons chili powder

1/2 teaspoon Celtic sea salt

1 teaspoon freshly ground cayenne pepper

## Star Thistle Gelato

In a high-speed blender, combine all the ingredients and process until smooth. Freeze in an ice-cream maker according to the manufacturer's directions. Use immediately, or store in the freezer for up to 2 weeks.

**Yield: 3 cups**

1 1/2 cups Cashew Milk (page 191)

1/2 cup coconut water

3/4 cup chopped young Thai coconut meat

6 tablespoons raw star thistle honey

3 tablespoons coconut oil

1/2 teaspoon seeds from vanilla bean

# Glossary of Ingredients and Techniques

AGAR-AGAR

A gelling agent extracted from a marine plant, agar-agar is available in three forms—powdered, sheets, and strands.

AMARANTH

An annual herb prized both for its broad green leaves and its seeds. The leaves taste somewhat like spinach and can be prepared in the same way, while the seeds are cooked like a grain or ground into flour.

ARBEQUINA OLIVE

A highly prized olive variety widely cultivated in Catalonia. The fruits are pressed to yield a particularly delicate and fruity oil and are cured for table use.

BARHI DATE

A relatively small, brown date with particularly sweet, moist flesh.

BATON

Matchstick-sized strip about 2 inches long by $1/8$ inch thick by $1/8$ inch wide.

BLACK MISSION FIG

Small, sweet fig with dark purple-black skin and tender, reddish flesh.

BLACK TRUMPET MUSHROOM

Also known as the trumpet of death for its dark color, this relatively small, delicately textured mushroom has a subtle smoky flavor.

BLEEDING HEART RADISH

A type of radish with green-pink skin, rosy flesh, and a taste that combines turnip and radish.

BROCCOFLOWER

A bright chartreuse member of the cabbage family, broccoflower looks like a cross between broccoli and cauliflower but is a variety of the latter. It has tight florets and a mild flavor.

BRUNOISE

Fine dice, about $1/8$ inch square.

CARDAMOM

Two types of cardamom are available, green and black. The green variety has a pale outer pod and tiny, dark seeds. Black cardamom has a dark, harder outer pod and larger, more aromatic seeds.

CAROB POWDER

The ground dried pulp from the pod of the tropical carob tree.

CAULIFLOWER MUSHROOM

An off-white mushroom that resembles a cauliflower head in appearance but not in taste. It has a tender, spongy texture and a mild mushroom flavor.

CELTIC SEA SALT

Naturally harvested, light gray sea salt from the Brittany coast of France. It is unrefined and has a high mineral content.

CHANTERELLE MUSHROOM

A mushroom with a lily shape and a heady aroma. Most common variety is orange-gold; other types include black, white, blue, and yellow footed.

CHIFFONADE

Fine strips usually about $1/16$ inch wide. The term is generally applied to the leaves of herbs or of leafy green vegetables, which are stacked, rolled up lengthwise, and then finely cut crosswise.

CHILE VINEGAR

White vinegar flavored with Thai chiles.

CINNAMON CAP MUSHROOM

Mild- and earthy-flavored mushroom with a small, orange-brown cap.

COCONUT BUTTER

Unrefined coconut oil in solid form. The nonhydrogenated oil, which is high in saturated fats, solidifies at temperatures below 85°F.

COCONUT WATER

The tasty, refreshing liquid inside a coconut. Look for young coconuts, which yield a greater amount of water, or juice, than older ones.

## DATE SUGAR
Unrefined sugar made by finely grinding dried dates.

## DINO KALE
A kale variety with narrow, dark green, crinkly leaves and a mild flavor. Also known as lacinato kale.

## ELEPHANT GARLIC
A member of the Allium family, and not a true garlic, elephant garlic has large cloves that are considerably milder than those of their smaller namesake.

## ENOKI MUSHROOM
A white mushroom with a thin, long stem, a tiny, white cap shaped like the head of a pin, a crisp texture, and a mild flavor.

## FERMENTED BLACK BEANS
Chinese black soybeans that have been preserved in salt and are sometimes flavored with dried orange peel. Also known as salted black beans.

## FIVE-SPICE POWDER
A blend of ground spices—typically star anise, clove, Sichuan pepper, cassia, and fennel—used primarily in southern China and Vietnam.

## FLEUR DE SEL
Light, snowy crystals of salt harvested along the coast of France through the natural evaporation of seawater.

## FRENCH MELON
A fragrant melon the size of a large orange with netted skin and a flavor similar to that of cantaloupe.

## GARAM MASALA
Literally "warm spice blend," garam masala is a ground mixture of such everyday Indian spices as clove, cardamom, cinnamon, pepper, and nutmeg.

## GARLIC SHOOT
Green shoot, or leaf, of the garlic plant that resembles a thick chive and has a mild garlic flavor.

## GOLDEN FLAXSEED

The tiny seed of a perennial herb prized for its healthful benefits and nutty flavor.

## GOLDEN FLAX MEAL

Finely ground golden flaxseed.

## GOOSEBERRY

A tart berry with green, white, golden, or red-black skin and a fleshy interior.

## GRAPESEED OIL

An oil of neutral flavor made by pressing grapeseeds.

## GREEN & BLACK'S ORGANIC COCOA POWDER

Unsweetened cocoa powder produced from organic beans, made by a premium British chocolate manufacturer.

## HIBISCUS LEAF

The leaf of the pink hibiscus plant. The dried leaves are commonly used for making tea, while the fresh leaves can be added to salads or soups or used as a garnish.

## HOJASANTA

A plant with large, green leaves that taste of anise and nutmeg. Also known as the root beer plant or Mexican pepper leaf.

## HONEY GRANULES

A natural, pale yellow granulated sweetener with a mild honey taste.

## HUCKLEBERRY

A relative of the blueberry, the blue-black huckleberry, also known as the whortleberry, is smaller and tarter than its kin and is not cultivated.

## INDIAN RED PEACH

An heirloom peach with rusty red skin and red flesh.

## KABOCHA SQUASH

A round winter squash with pale orange flesh and bright green skin with pale green stripes.

## KELP GRANULES

Sea kelp that has been chopped, dried, and finely ground to saltlike granules.

## KEY LIME
A round, yellow-green fruit about one-fourth the size of the more common Persian lime and with a tarter flavor.

## KOHLRABI
A relative of the turnip, kohlrabi is cultivated primarily for its thickened, bulbous stem, which has a mild turnip flavor and a firm texture. The leaves are also edible.

## LEMON VERBENA
Sometimes called simply verbena, an herb with a pronounced lemon flavor. The leaves are long and narrow and have saw-toothed edges.

## LE PLUS ALMONDS
A heirloom variety of raw almond. Other whole raw almonds can be substituted.

## LIME RADISH
A type of radish with white-green skin and white flesh marked with a green ring near the exterior wall. It has a taste that combines radish and turnip.

## LONGAN
Native to China, the longan is a small, round fruit with a thin, hard, easily removable shell, translucent white flesh, and a single black seed.

## MAMEY SAPOTE
A large, elongated tropical fruit with rough brown skin, fragrant yellow-orange flesh, and a single large, brown pit.

## MAPLE SUGAR
A moist pure sugar made by reducing maple syrup until it crystallizes.

## MEDJOOL DATE
A large, dark purplish-red, meaty date with an especially full flavor.

## MEXICAN TARRAGON
Anise-scented herb with a flavor and leaf shape similar to that of French tarragon. Although a member of the same family as its French namesake, it belongs to a different genus. Also known as Mexican mint marigold.

## MISO
Two types of Japanese miso are used in this book, white miso and barley miso. The former is made by combining soybeans and rice and allowing them to ferment to create a mild, pale paste. The latter mixes the soybeans with barley in place of the rice. Both are available in sweet and salty forms; use the latter for the recipes in this book.

## NAMA SHOYU
Ohsawa brand raw (unpasteurized) organic soy sauce made from soybeans and wheat. It is aged for four years and is made with less salt than traditional soy sauce.

## NUTRITIONAL YEAST
Yeast grown specifically for its nutritional benefits, among which are high levels of protein and B-complex vitamins.

## OPAL BASIL
A variety of basil with purple leaves and a mild clove flavor.

## ORANGE CHERRY PEPPER
An orange pepper than resembles a sweet pimiento pepper in size, shape, and flavor.

## PASSION FRUIT
A small, oval tropical fruit with a hard outer shell and gold-orange pulp punctuated with many tiny, black seeds.

## PEPITA
Mexican term for pumpkin seed. Look for dried raw seeds with their white hulls removed.

## POM POM MUSHROOM
Mild, white mushroom that grows in clusters on the branches of conifers. It is often dried and can be rehydrated quickly in water.

## QUENELLE
Traditionally refers to an oval dumpling made from a forcemeat of fish, veal, or poultry, but can be used for any food formed into small ovals.

## RAPINI
Also known as broccoli rabe, rapini, with its slender stalk, small florets, jagged-edged leaves, and bright green color, resembles a slim head of broccoli.

## RED ORACH SPROUTS

Sprouts grown from the seeds of red orach, a purple-leaved green vegetable with a mild flavor.

## REJUVELAC

The fermented liquid that is drained from sprouted grains, usually rye or wheat berries. You can make your own (see Basic Recipes), or you can purchase it at a health-food store.

## SALSIFY

A long, thin root vegetable, the most common type of which has charcoal skin and white flesh. Also know as oyster plant because of its mild oysterlike flavor.

## SEA BEAN

A sea vegetable, also known as samphire or glasswort, with pointed, rodlike, fleshy green leaves that give the plant the look of a cactus. It has a pleasantly salty taste and a crisp texture.

## SESAME OIL

Clear, mild, nutty-tasting oil made from sesame seeds. Look for oil that has been cold-pressed without the aid of chemicals. There is also toasted sesame oil, in which the seeds are roasted before pressing to produce a nuttier taste and a rich brown color. Chile-infused sesame oil is oil in which Thai chiles have steeped.

## SHARLYN MELON

An oval melon with netted skin and sweet, fragrant, nearly white flesh. The Sharlyn is highly perishable, and once ripe, its flesh will begin to break down within a couple of days. Cantaloupe or Crenshaw can be substituted.

## SHISO

The saw-toothed leaf of the perilla plant. There are two types, green shiso, which has a tangy lemon-mint flavor and is the most common, and red shiso, which is milder.

## SMOKED SALT

There are several commercial smoked salts on the market. You can also attempt to smoke your own salt by placing Celtic sea salt or fleur de sel in an open heatproof container in a cold smoker, although the commercial brands are superior.

## SPROUTED FLOUR

This product has been developed for retail sale by Roxanne's restaurant. To purchase, call 415.924.5004 or visit www.roxraw.com.

## SPROUTED MEAL

This product has been developed for retail sale by Roxanne's restaurant. To purchase, call 415.924.5004 or visit www.roxraw.com.

## STAR FRUIT

A yellow-green tropical fruit with an elongated body and five deep ridges running its length. When cut crosswise, the fruit yields slices in the shape of a five-pointed star, thus the name. The sweet-sour fruit has crisp flesh. Also known as carambola.

## SUIZENJI NORI

A type of Japanese freshwater alga available dried in thin sheets.

## SUPREMED

Used to describe a citrus segment from which the white membrane and pith have been removed.

## TAHINI

Rich, thick paste made from ground sesame seeds. Use only raw tahini, rather than the toasted variety.

## TENGUSA SEAWEED

Also known as heavenly grass, this Japanese seaweed with gelatinlike properties is often used to make agar-agar. It is beige, has a mild flavor, and is sold dried.

## THAI BASIL

A variety of basil with a purple stem, small green leaves, and a mild anise flavor.

## THAI COCONUT

Also known as young Thai coconuts, these coconuts are harvested at between six and nine months, have soft meat, and often contain as much as 3 cups of coconut water. Once the coconuts begin to age, the meat starts to harden and the water slowly evaporates. Look for Thai coconuts in Asian markets, where they are usually trimmed to resemble a spinning top and have a soft, white husk.

## THAI DRAGON CHILE

A red chile about 3 inches long and six times hotter than a jalapeño.

## THAI LIME LEAF

Widely used in Thai cuisine, this wonderfully fragrant, flavorful leaf is deep green and has a glossy sheen.

## TRUFFLE OIL

Olive oil that has been infused with black or white truffles.

## VILLA MANODORI BALSAMIC VINEGAR

A celebrated artisanal balsamic vinegar produced in limited quantities in Modena, Italy. It is made from Trebbiano grapes and is aged in oak, chestnut, and juniper barrels.

## WAKAME SEAWEED

A type of brown alga that is usually available dried in bundled strands. Appreciated for its superior flavor and texture.

## WASABI

A Japanese herb used primarily for its root, which is peeled and grated to yield a pungent, pale green paste.

## WHITE SHOYU

Soy sauce made with a larger proportion of wheat than regular shoyu.

## WINGED BEAN

A pale green tropical bean with four ridged fins running the length of its pod. It has a starchy, mild taste and is a rich source of protein.

## WOLFBERRY

Small, red berry native to China. Sold dried, the wolfberry is appreciated for its many healthful benefits and its pleasant taste.

## YUZU CITRON

A Japanese citron about the size of a tangerine that is most commonly used for its aromatic rind. The juice is made by pressing the whole fruit—rind and pulp.

# Index

**1 ☉ TEN SPEED PRESS**

Box 7123  Berkeley, California 94707  www.tenspeed.com

Distributed in Australia by Simon & Schuster Australia, in Canada by
Ten Speed Press Canada, in New Zealand by Southern Publishers Group,
in South Africa by Real Books, and in the United Kingdom and Europe
by Airlift Book Company.

Developmental editor: Sharon Silva
Editor: Aaron Wehner, Ten Speed Press
Research, development, and recipe testing: Sari Zernich, Charlie Trotter's
Recipe testing and development: Stephanie Valentine, Roxanne's
Recipe testing: Guillermo Tellez, Charlie Trotter's
Graphic design and typesetting: Three Communication Design (3CD)

Library of Congress Cataloging-in-Publication Data

Trotter, Charlie.
    Raw / by Charlie Trotter and Roxanne Klein; wine notes by Jason Smith;
photography by Tim Turner.
        p. cm.
Includes index.
    ISBN 1-58008-470-2
    1. Vegetarian cookery. 2. Raw foods. I. Klein, Roxanne. II. Title.
TX837 .T783 2003
641.5636--dc22

                                                    2003018075

Printed in Canada
First printing, 2003

1 2 3 4 5 6 7 8 9 10 — 07 06 05 04 03